CUSTER
A Photographic Biography

Bill & Jan Moeller

2003 • MOUNTAIN PRESS PUBLISHING COMPANY • Missoula, Montana

Cover image: "Sighting the Enemy" by Edward Potter, Monroe, Michigan

Library of Congress Cataloging-in-Publication Date
    Moeller, Bill, 1930-
      Custer : a photographic biography / Bill and Jan Moeller.
         p. cm.
    Rev. ed. of: Custer, his life, his adventures. c1988.
    Includes bibliographical references and index.
      ISBN 0-87842-483-0 (pbk. : alk. paper)
    1. Custer, George Armstrong, 1839-1876. 2. Custer, George Armstrong,
1839-1876—Pictorial works. 3. Generals—United States—Biography. 4. Generals—
United States—Pictorial works. 5. UnitedStates—History—Civil War, 1861-1865—
Pictorial works. 6. Indians of North America—Wars—1866-1895—Pictorial works.
7. United States Army—Biography. I. Moeller, Jan, 1930- II. Moeller, Bill, 1930-
Custer, his life, his adventures. III. Title.
      E467.1.C99M63 2003
      973.8'2'092—dc22
                           2003017387

Printed in Hong Kong by Mantec Production Company

Mountain Press Publishing Company
P. O. Box 2399 • Missoula, MT 59806
(406) 728-1900 • fax (406) 728-1635

Contents

Introduction

George Armstrong Custer—the very mention of the name brings forth strong emotions in many people even now, more than a century after his death. His detractors are many, and their accounts of his life often contain legends, misconceptions, and half-truths.

Yet even some of his detractors would have to admit Custer was a remarkable leader. In most cases he could size up a situation instantly and do whatever was necessary to turn it to his advantage. During the Civil War, his men adored him for his bravery and daring. Although he could be as stern a disciplinarian as any officer when necessary, Custer was always concerned about the well-being and morale of his troops, making sure they were well fed and adequately supplied. When things were going badly or when boredom set in, he tried to buoy their spirits with positive words and an upbeat attitude. Custer was known for his sense of humor and was quite a practical joker, and he had the ability to laugh at his own mistakes.

Custer neither smoked nor drank, and he did not tolerate drunkenness in his command. Some of his bitterest enemies were those he punished for being drunk on duty. But he was not vindictive. In fact he forbade his wife, Libbie, from openly speaking ill of his critics and instructed her to always treat them graciously.

Custer was also a devoted husband. The relationship between him and his wife is one of the great love stories of all time. The two were never happy apart; Libbie joined her husband whenever possible, uncomplainingly enduring any hardship to be with him. When the Custers were separated, they exchanged frequent, lengthy letters. Custer sometimes wrote Libbie more than once a day, and one of his letters was forty-two pages long.

Custer was close to his family and regularly corresponded with his half-sister, Lydia Reed. He had an almost paternal interest in the doings of his nieces and nephew. One of his brothers, Boston, and his nephew, Autie Reed, were with him and died at the Little Bighorn, as was his sister Maggie's husband, James Calhoun.

Although much has been written about Custer—some of it containing not only distortions but outright lies—we think there is always room for a different approach to a subject. In this book we have tried to present a balanced, factual account of the life of this controversial figure. Recounting his story mainly through photographs—another way in which this book is different from other Custer biographies—with every significant place in his life represented, we hope this book will offer readers a window into Custer's world, through which we may see him less as either hero or villain, and more as simply a man.

Custer farm, New Rumley, Ohio

~ One ~

THE EARLY YEARS
December 1839 to April 1861

December 5, 1839

George Armstrong Custer was born in New Rumley, Ohio, the first child of Emmanuel Custer and his second wife, Maria Ward Kirkpatrick. Emmanuel was a blacksmith and also a member of the local militia. During his childhood, Autie, as his family called him, often watched his father drill with his militia company, introducing the youngster to military life. In helping his father in the blacksmith shop adjacent to the house, Autie also learned to handle horses. Emmanuel, an outspoken Democrat with Southern sympathies, influenced his son's later political philosophy.

Raisin River, Monroe, Michigan

December 1849

When Autie was ten years old, his parents sent him to live with his half-sister, Lydia Ann, and her husband, David Reed, in Monroe, Michigan, believing he could get a better education there. Although the boy despised studying, he was intelligent and learned quickly.

June 1856

When Custer was sixteen, he returned to Harrison County, Ohio, and began teaching at the Beach Point and Locust Grove schools. Between terms he attended the McNeely Normal School in Hopedale, Ohio, for teacher training. During this time he boarded with the Holland family and became enamored of their daughter, Mary, who was near his own age. He even asked her father for her hand, but Mr. Holland opposed the match and withheld his consent.

Soon after this, Custer decided to apply to West Point. He wrote to John H. Bingham, his congressional representative, requesting an appointment to the academy, but he learned that the appointment for that year had been filled. Bingham, a Republican, was not disposed to doing favors for southern Democrats, but Holland, also a Republican and a prominent farmer, may have interceded on Custer's behalf. After all, Custer's attendance at West Point would keep him away from Mary and forestall their potential marriage. In January 1857, Custer received notification that he had been accepted at West Point.

1857 to 1861

With his irrepressible sense of humor, Custer was well-liked by his classmates. Because of his long blond curls, they nicknamed him "Fanny." He shared a room in the Tower Barracks with Jim Parker, a Kentuckian, and many of his close friends were from the South.

On April 12, 1861, the Confederates fired on Fort Sumter, South Carolina, beginning the Civil War. Many of Custer's friends resigned from West Point and enlisted in the Confederate Army. Knowing Custer's Southern sympathies, some of these friends urged him to join the Confederates, but he decided that a country that had provided him with such a fine education deserved his loyalty, so he chose to fight for the Union.

Because both armies needed trained officers, all the cadets who were to graduate in 1862, including Custer, received their diplomas a year early. The new Lieutenant Custer was ordered to leave immediately for Washington, D.C., and report to his regiment, Company G of the Second United States Cavalry.

Tower Barracks, West Point. Custer's room
was in a similar building, no longer standing.

Hudson River from the United States Military Academy, West Point, New York

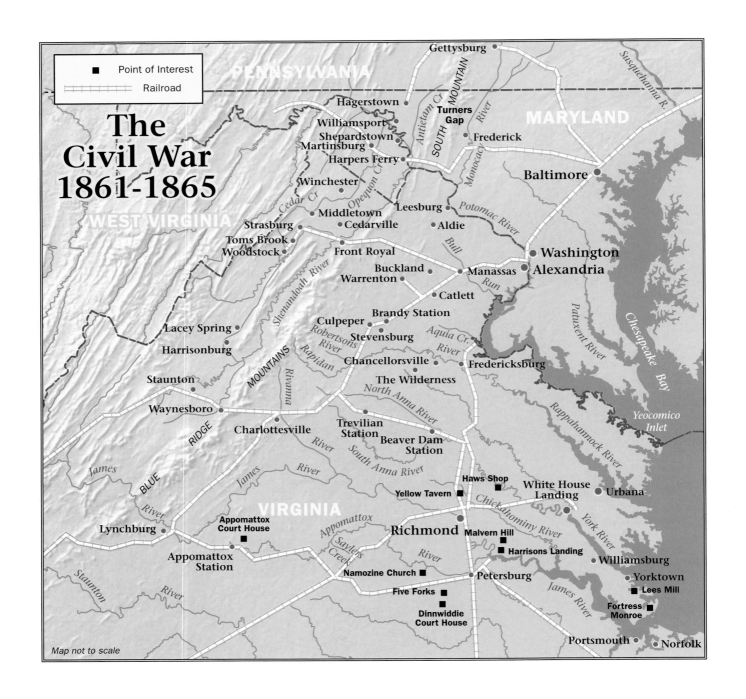

The Civil War 1861-1865

Point of Interest

Railroad

Map not to scale

PENNSYLVANIA

MARYLAND

WEST VIRGINIA

VIRGINIA

Gettysburg

Hagerstown

Turners Gap

SOUTH MOUNTAIN

Antietam Cr

Frederick

Williamsport
Shepardstown
Martinsburg
Harpers Ferry

Winchester

Monocacy River

Baltimore

Cedar Cr

Opequon Cr

Middletown

Leesburg

Potomac River

Susquehanna R.

Strasburg
Toms Brook
Woodstock

Cedarville

Aldie

Front Royal

Shenandoah River

Buckland
Warrenton

Manassas

Bull Run

Washington
Alexandria

Catlett

Lacey Spring

Harrisonburg

MOUNTAINS

Rivanna

Rapidan

Robertsons River

Culpeper

Stevensburg

Brandy Station

Aquia Cr. River

Chancellorsville

Fredericksburg

Patuxent River

Chesapeake Bay

Staunton

The Wilderness

North Anna River

Rappahannock River

Yeocomico Inlet

Waynesboro

BLUE RIDGE

Charlottesville

River

James River

Trevilian Station

Beaver Dam Station

South Anna River

Haws Shop

Yellow Tavern

White House Landing

Urbana

James River

Chickahominy River

York River

Lynchburg

Appomattox Court House

Appomattox River

Saylers Creek

Richmond

Malvern Hill

Harrisons Landing

Williamsburg

Yorktown

Lees Mill

Appomattox Station

Namozine Church

Petersburg

James River

Fortress Monroe

Staunton River

Five Forks

Dinnwiddie Court House

Portsmouth

Norfolk

Two

MAKING A NAME FOR HIMSELF
July 1861 to June 1863

July 21, 1861

Custer's first engagement in the war was near the town of Manassas, Virginia, less than thirty miles from Washington. Union troops were to stop the Confederates from marching on the capital city. By 10 A.M. on July 21, Custer's company was in position to protect the artillery emplacement commanded by Lt. Charles Griffin. The artillery was deployed on a ridge north of the Confederate main line, which was along the west side of the stream known as Bull Run. The cavalry was sequestered in a hollow, out of sight.

Custer and a fellow officer, Lieutenant Walker, were apprehensive about what their first battle would bring. Walker wondered whether to use his saber or pistol in the expected charge. In response, Custer pulled his pistol from its holster, put it right back and

grasped his saber, changed back to the pistol, then again to the saber. Walker watched, bewildered, until he realized his comrade was putting him on. They shared a good laugh, easing the tension. The choice of weapon turned out to be moot—the infantry drove the Rebels back onto Henry Hill without help from the cavalry.

In midafternoon, following Griffin's artillery, the cavalry advanced only a short distance before it was ordered to halt and wait in a sheltered place, from which the men could not see what was going on. On Henry Hill, the Northerners were having a hard time against the brigade of Brig. Gen. Thomas J. Jackson, who won the nickname "Stonewall" in this battle. Just when the Union troops had driven the Rebels back, a new column of Confederates

Henry Hill, Manassas National Battlefield Park, Manassas, Virginia

emerged from the woods on their right and flanked them.

By four o'clock, after fighting for fourteen hours, the exhausted Union forces began to crumble. The men began to fall back, and before long, the Federal troops fled in a disorganized retreat over the stone bridge on the road back to Washington. The Confederates, satisfied with their victory, did not pursue them. Custer was bewildered by the retreat and speculated that if the cavalry had been called upon to fight, the battle at Bull Run might have ended differently. During the retreat, Custer was instrumental in keeping his comrades from panicking, and he received a citation for his actions.

Henry Hill

October 1861 to February 1862

Because it was winter, Custer saw no action during the seven months after the battle at Bull Run. In October he took a sick leave and went home to Michigan. There he discovered his presence at Bull Run had made him something of a hero to the townspeople.

While he was home, Elizabeth Bacon, the comely daughter of Judge Daniel Stanton Bacon, caught Custer's eye. They had known each other by sight since childhood, but they moved in different social circles, and Custer was unable to introduce himself before he left to rejoin his regiment in February.

March 14, 1862

By the time Custer returned to duty, the Confederates had withdrawn from Manassas and pulled back to Richmond, and the Union army had been reorganized under Maj. Gen. George McClellan. Custer was reassigned to the Fifth Cavalry, which was ordered to advance to Richmond.

At Catlett, a railroad station fifteen miles southwest of Manassas Junction, Custer's regiment received orders to drive back some Rebel pickets, and Custer volunteered his company. His request granted, the company made a saber charge and pushed the Confederates back over the bridge across Cedar Run.

The Fifth Cavalry's march to Richmond was actually a feint to determine the number of Confederate troops in the vicinity of Washington, D.C. After learning that the Southern force there was too small to threaten the capital, McClellan planned a campaign to attack Richmond from the southeast. He ordered his troops onto ships headed down the Chesapeake Bay to Fortress Monroe in Hampton, Virginia.

Cedar Run, south of Catlett, Virginia

April 7 to May 4, 1862

Now McClellan was ready to move on Richmond, intending to go up the peninsula between the York and James Rivers. Sixty miles southeast of Richmond, the Union forces encountered Confederate troops entrenched on the west side of the Warwick River at Lees Mill. Custer was ordered to go up in a balloon to determine the strength of the enemy. He suggested the ascents be made at night; that way he would not be seen but could ascertain the number and placement of the Rebels from their campfires.

On the night of May 4, Custer saw no campfires. The next morning he volunteered to cross the river to see whether the Rebels were gone, and he found that they were. After sporadic artillery and rifle fire and a brief Union assault on Confederate rifle pits across the river, no further action took place at Lee's Mill.

Approximate site of Lees Mill, Newport News City Park, Newport News, Virginia

Williamsburg, Virginia

Skiff Creek, near Williamsburg, Virginia

May 5, 1862

As the Union army advanced up the peninsula toward Williamsburg, Custer's company was at the head of the column in the brigade of Brig. Gen. Winfield Scott Hancock. When they arrived at the bridge over Skiff Creek, they found that the Rebels had set it on fire. In putting out the flames with some of his men, Custer burned his hands.

Moving north, the brigade captured three small redoubts before coming upon a larger one that was heavily manned. Hancock ordered a bayonet charge, and Custer volunteered to lead it. But the troopers, many of them unseasoned, were slow to follow. Displaying the style for which he later became famous, Custer rode back and forth before the men, waving his hat, joking, and encouraging them on. Energized, the cheering blue line drove back the Rebels, and the redoubt soon fell into Union hands. By nightfall on May 5, the Union army was camped in Williamsburg. Custer received two citations for his actions in the engagement.

May 23, 1862

McClellan's army advanced without incident far up the peninsula. The general established his headquarters near the Chickahominy River, less than ten miles from Richmond. Custer was sent on many scouting trips in the area. On one of them, Brig. Gen. John G. Barnard ordered Custer to wade into the Chickahominy to determine its depth. Holding his pistol above his head to keep it dry, Custer strode in. When he reached the far bank, Barnard signaled him to come back, but Custer ignored him; instead, he carefully and quietly crawled through the underbrush and discovered a well-concealed Rebel picket post in a bend of the river.

Recrossing the river, Custer told Barnard where the pickets were, and Barnard immediately reported the information to McClellan. The general asked to meet the soldier who had shown such initiative. When the muddy and bedraggled lieutenant appeared before him, McClellan asked him to join his staff. Astounded, Custer barely managed to stammer his acceptance.

The next day, Custer led a company to capture the post he had discovered. Shortly afterward he was promoted to brevet captain.

Chickahominy River east of Mechanicsville, Virginia

June 27, 1862

After McClellan received captured documents indicating that the Confederates were about to attack, he split his forces and placed troops on both sides of the Chickahominy River, which was severely flooded from recent heavy rains. Rebel general Robert E. Lee recognized an excellent opportunity to attack while the army was divided. He threw the bulk of his forces against Maj. Gen. Fitz-John Porter's Fifth Corps, who were protecting the Union's northern supply line, which originated at White House Landing on the York River.

McClellan asked Custer if he knew a way to get through to the beleagured Porter. The captain thought he could reach him via the Grapevine Bridge over the Chickahominy. McClellan gave Custer two brigades, and Custer led them to Porter's position. With the fresh troops aiding him, Porter retreated to safety.

Grapevine Bridge site, Chickahominy River east of Richmond, Virginia

July 1, 1862

After Porter's retreat, the Rebels cut off McClellan's supply line. It was imperative that the general establish another immediately. Choosing a point on the James River as the new base, he moved his troops south. As they retreated, the Unionists faced constant Confederate harassment. McClellan decided to stop and fight at Malvern Hill. The Rebels delayed attacking until midafternoon, giving the Yankee general plenty of time to place his artillery advantageously.

In the wait before the battle, Custer did some harassing of his own. Accompanied by their orderlies, he and a lieutenant flushed out a small Rebel patrol. The Confederates surrendered their guns and sabers to Custer, but with the enemy's line now advancing so rapidly, all Custer could do was take the Rebels' arms and run. The four arrived back at the Union line laughing in triumph, loaded down with the captured weapons.

The battle at Malvern Hill turned out to be indecisive.

Malvern Hill, Richmond National Battlefield Park, Richmond, Virginia

August 10, 1862

McClellan established his new supply base at Harrison's Landing on the James River. From there, Custer was sent on an expedition to White Oak Swamp, not far to the north, where his party clashed with a small group of Confederates. A Rebel officer led Custer on a wild chase. Twice Custer called to him to surrender. When he did not, Custer shot him. Shortly he came upon the officer's riderless horse and claimed it, along with its magnificent silver-studded morocco saddle and the fine sword hanging from it.

White Oak Swamp, north of Hopewell, Virginia

August 20, 1862

By mid-August, with most of the Union troops deployed elsewhere, Washington, D.C., was nearly defenseless. A worried President Abraham Lincoln ordered McClellan's army to return to the area. McClellan reached Fortress Monroe without incident. On the way, Custer stopped in Williamsburg to see his friend and West Point classmate Gimlet Lea, a Confederate soldier. Custer had been in Williamsburg the previous May and had discovered Lea in a barn there, wounded and a Union prisoner.

Lea was now recuperating at Bassett Hall, the home of Mrs. Goodrich Durfey, and had become engaged to her daughter. Lea asked Custer to be best man at his wedding, which was only a few days away. Custer received leave to attend, and afterward he hurried to rejoin McClellan in Washington.

Bassett Hall, Williamsburg, Virginia

Turners Gap, South Mountain, east of Boonsboro, Maryland

Near Boonsboro, Maryland

September 14, 1862

McClellan had established his headquarters at Rockville, Maryland, a few miles northwest of Washington, and Custer reported there for duty. After a Confederate victory at the Second Battle of Bull Run on August 30, General Lee intended to invade Maryland, but the Yankees captured a dispatch that revealed the plan to McClellan. To intercept the Rebels, the Union army had to cross South Mountain, a one-thousand-foot-high ridge with only two main gaps.

Custer was sent to Turners Gap, the one farther north, to join Brig. Gen. Alfred Pleasonton. Rebel troops met them at the summit, and the two armies fought along the ridge until nightfall. At that point it was unclear who had won. The next morning, Custer and the cavalry made their way down the western slope of the mountain in a dense fog. Breaking through the fog at last near the town of Boonsboro, they saw Lee's army retreating. Custer and a few other cavalrymen fired at the Confederate lines from behind some stone fences, but Lee's men ignored them and marched on.

On the way back to Gen. Pleasonton, Custer rounded up two Rebel cannons and several hundred Confederate soldiers who had been lagging behind. He was given another merit citation.

Pry House, Antietam National Battlefield, Sharpsburg, Maryland

Antietam Battlefield, looking northwest

September 17, 1862

Union leaders expected Lee to retreat across the Potomac River, but instead he halted at Sharpsburg, Maryland, midway between the river and Antietam Creek. McClellan, in pursuit, planned his strategy from the Pry House, just below a ridge on the east side of the creek. He wanted to attack both the right and left of the Southerners' line, then charge the middle, which would by then be weakened. McClellan's force outnumbered Lee's two-to-one, so the plan should have worked, but, characteristically, McClellan moved too slowly and lost the chance for decisive victory.

That day at Antietam was the bloodiest day of the war. Yet the only action Custer saw was through field glasses from headquarters, where he stayed with McClellan. The fighting stopped at nightfall. The next day found both sides waiting for the other to resume the battle, but, with casualties so high and the men exhausted, neither did. On September 18, in darkness, Lee withdrew his army across the Potomac.

Winter 1862-63

Custer spent most of the winter on leave in Michigan, except for several weeks in January when, ordered to Trenton, New Jersey, he helped General McClellan write his memoirs. McClellan had been relieved as commander of the Army of the Potomac in the autumn of 1862 after his failure at Antietam.

In Monroe at a Thanksgiving party, Custer was formally introduced to Elizabeth Bacon, or Libbie, as she was called. He was immediately smitten, but Libbie, who had many beaus, was indifferent to Custer. Nevertheless, over the winter, Custer managed to squire her to many social functions. Eventually she warmed to him and he became her most frequent escort.

Judge Bacon was impressed with Custer's war exploits, but because the young man came from a poor family he did not look upon him as an acceptable suitor for his daughter. After several months of courtship, the judge forbade Libbie to see Custer or even to write to him when he left. Libbie would not disobey her father, but she got around the restriction by telling Custer to write to her friend Nettie Humphrey. Thus began quite a correspondence between Custer and Nettie.

May 19, 1863

When Lieutenant Custer (he lost his captaincy when McClellan lost his command) returned to his company, he had been assigned to serve under Pleasonton, who held the newly created post of Chief of Cavalry. Custer was to be Pleasonton's aide-de-camp. His first assignment was to lead an amphibious raid deep into Rebel territory and intercept some Southern civilians carrying important mail and a large sum of money.

Custer took his men and their horses aboard two steamboats on Aquia Creek, and they sailed down the Potomac and the Chesapeake Bay to Yeocomico Inlet. From there, the party went overland to the Rappahannock River. In two captured boats, they crossed over to Urbanna, Virginia, where they burned a bridge and two schooners, confiscated crates of Confederate supplies, and captured four Rebel soldiers and thirty horses. Custer found the civilians he was looking for on a sailboat on the Rappahannock. He forced their boat ashore and took them back to Union headquarters for questioning.

Rappahannock River, Urbanna, Virginia

June 9, 1863

Maj. Gen. Joseph Hooker, McClellan's replacement as commander of the Army of the Potomac, ordered Pleasonton to probe into central Virginia to find out where Lee's army was headed. Before dawn on June 9, Pleasonton sent Custer with the Eighth New York Cavalry under Col. Benjamin F. Davis to cross the Rappahannock River at Beverly Ford, six miles east of Brandy Station. After plowing through the Confederate sentry post on the west bank, the Union troopers charged into a thousand Rebels having their breakfast. The Southerners, unorganized and unhorsed, surrendered without a fight. They were part of the ten-thousand-man force known as the Invincibles, under Maj. Gen. J.E.B. "Jeb" Stuart.

Nearby, the Northerners noticed gray-coated cavalrymen—more of Stuart's men—organizing in a field behind a stone fence. The Eighth Illinois and the Third Indiana Cavalry had arrived and joined Davis's regiment, and together Davis and Custer led a charge over the fence, driving the Rebels into the woods beyond. During the charge, Davis was shot and Custer took command. Finding himself surrounded, he ordered a halt, re-formed the men, and led a saber charge back through the enemy. At that point, Custer saw that the Confederate line had diminished. He kept up a steady harassment of the thinning ranks until they were completely dispersed.

Around noon, Custer's force joined Pleasonton's, and together they pushed on to Brandy Station. But more Confederate troops came onto the field, and Pleasonton ordered the Union men back across the Rappahannock.

West of Beverly Ford on the Rappahannock River and east of Brandy Station, Virginia

June 17, 1863

Lee, still trying to move the war into the North, was heading for Pennsylvania. His army stretched out for many miles across Virginia. Stuart's cavalry, on the right flank, was to act as a buffer against Union forces. Hooker sent Pleasonton to ferret out the weak spots in the long Confederate line.

Custer was attached to the brigade of Col. Hugh Judson Kilpatrick. Just north of the village of Aldie, about midway between Manassas and Leesburg, Kilpatrick's troops encountered Stuart's cavalry, positioned behind rocks and stone fences on either side of a four-gun battery. With two regiments, Kilpatrick led a charge against the line. When the colonel's horse was shot from under him, Custer assumed command, continued the charge, and broke through.

Suddenly Custer, in the lead, found himself alone and surrounded by the enemy. Because he wore a broad-brimmed "slouch" hat, a style favored by Southerners, he was evidently mistaken for one of them, and he got away before his identity was discovered.

North of Aldie, Virginia

June 26, 1863

When Pleasonton was promoted to major general in early June, Custer became a captain. In the past, Custer had remarked to his friends that everyone seemed to be getting promotions except him, but he said he intended to be a general before the war was over.

Because Lee was advancing into Pennsylvania, Pleasonton's corps and others were sent to Frederick, Maryland. On the rainy day of June 26, Custer had been out in the mud overseeing the placement of sentries around Pleasonton's headquarters. When he arrived back at his quarters, he was greeted with shouts of "Hello, General!" Custer thought he was being ribbed until his comrades pointed to an envelope on the table addressed to Brigadier General George A. Custer, U.S. Volunteers. The twenty-three-year-old was speechless.

After Custer recovered his wits and accepted his fellow officers' congratulations, he called his orderly, Joseph Fought, to help him assemble a uniform to indicate his new rank. Fought found two gold stars and sewed them to the large collar points of a sailor shirt Custer often wore. From a peddler, Fought purchased a loose, black velveteen jacket with sleeves trimmed with loops of gold braid reaching to the elbows. Custer wore the jacket over the shirt with the collar points showing on the outside. A bright red tie finished off the ensemble. In this makeshift uniform with the highly visible stars, Custer figured there would be no doubt about his rank.

Custer's new command was the Second Brigade of the Third Cavalry Division, which consisted of the First, Fifth, Sixth, and Seventh Michigan Volunteer Cavalry Regiments and Battery M of the Second U.S. Artillery. Known as the Michigan Brigade—or the Wolverines, after the state's nickname—the unit included many men from Custer's hometown of Monroe. On June 29, arrayed in his new uniform, which he topped off with his Confederate slouch hat, Custer set out to join his command, forty-five miles north near the Pennsylvania border.

Street scene, Frederick, Maryland

— Three —

"OLD CURLY"
July 1863 to June 1864

July 2, 1863

Hugh Judson Kilpatrick was now a brigadier general and commander of the Third Cavalry Division, which included Custer's Second Brigade. On July 2, Kilpatrick received orders to move toward Gettysburg as quickly as possible. Union and Confederate forces had engaged there the day before. General Lee was on the field, as was Maj. Gen. George G. Meade, who had recently replaced Hooker as Union commander. When Kilpatrick reached Meade's rear, General Pleasonton ordered him to place his men on the Union's right to protect it from being flanked.

As the troops moved into position, Custer sighted what he thought were about two hundred Confederate skirmishers. He immediately deployed along the road Battery M, under Lt. Alexander Pennington, and all his own companies except for Company A of the Fifth Michigan, which he placed in a line across the road as the vanguard of the attack. Custer galloped ahead of Company A, shouting, "I'll lead you this time, boys. Come on!" This was something the troops had never seen before—a general leading a single company in a charge. Cheering, they enthusiastically followed the dashing young man in his flamboyant uniform.

The charge, which turned out to be against Wade Hampton's entire brigade, did not repulse the enemy, but it stopped them from advancing. Custer was able to hold the field because of the good work of Pennington's battery. However, the fight—Custer's first as a general—left him sick at heart: Half the men in his company had been killed. He felt he had been careless in his initial assessment and blamed himself for the losses.

Pennington's battery location, cavalry battlefield, Gettysburg National Military Park

July 3, 1863

At Gettysburg, at 11 P.M. on July 2, Kilpatrick was ordered to move his division to the left of the Union line. Through most of the night, Custer and his men marched south. At dawn, after less than two hours' rest, Custer received orders from Second Cavalry Division commander Brig. Gen. David McMurtrie Gregg to bring his brigade back to where they had started the night before. The tired Michigan Brigade joined Gregg late in the morning.

In midafternoon, after an earlier brief artillery engagement by both sides, an extended line of gray-coated skirmishers from Jeb Stuart's cavalry emerged from the woods opposite the Fifth Michigan. The Union men were ordered to hold their fire until the Confederates were within 120 yards. Then the Fifth cut loose with a volley from their seven-shot Spencer repeating carbines.

After several volleys, the Fifth ran low on ammunition and were ordered to retire. Stuart assumed the Yanks were retreating and charged them. Now Custer, leading the Michiganders, rallied his men for a saber charge, shouting, "Come on, you Wolverines!" After two hours of close fighting, during which the seventh Michigan arrived, the Yanks eventually drove the Rebels back.

At four o'clock, an entire brigade of Confederates formed in close rank for a final charge while Custer was regrouping his troops. Only one full regiment, the veteran First, was available to counter the charge. After Battery M fired a withering volley of canister into the Confederate line, Custer again led the charge, urging on his Wolverines. They stopped the massive Southern force cold, and Stuart withdrew his bloodied troops from the field.

That night, Lee started his troops toward the Potomac, and Meade claimed a victory at Gettysburg, due in no small part to the actions of the cavalry that fought some three miles east of the main battlefield.

From J.E.B. Stuart's position on cavalry battlefield, Gettysburg National Military Park, Gettysburg, Pennsylvania

July 14, 1863

After Gettysburg, Lee moved his weary troops, in a column stretching for seventeen miles, southwest through Maryland toward the Potomac River, where he intended to cross into West Virgina and go on to the relative safety of Virginia. Along the way, Custer constantly harassed Lee's men. Every day for nine days, the Union soldiers skirmished with the retreating Army of Northern Virginia.

In Maryland, on the road to the Potomac crossing at Falling Waters, West Virginia, a significant battle occurred. Lee had ordered a pontoon bridge built at the crossing. To protect it he had placed a division along the road and on an adjacent hill. The Rebels were firmly entrenched.

Custer came upon Lee's division with only a squadron—two companies—from his brigade; the rest of the brigade was mopping up and gathering prisoners along the way. Custer had just ordered his dismounted men to advance slowly on the enemy when General Kilpatrick arrived on the scene. Having no perception of the Confederate strength, and taking no time to ascertain it, Kilpatrick rashly ordered the squadron to mount and charge. The resulting losses were heavy.

Another unit, the Sixth Michigan, arrived. Custer sent them, dismounted, to divert the entrenched Confederates until the rest of the brigade came up. When the reinforcements arrived, they were immediately thrown into the intense battle. By the end of the day, all the Confederates on the north side of the Potomac had been either driven across the river into West Virginia, taken prisoner, or killed. Against almost four times their number, the lone Michigan Brigade had taken fifteen hundred prisoners, two artillery pieces, and three battle flags.

Near Potomac River, south of Williamsport, Maryland

August 1863

After the Gettysburg operation, "Old Curly," as Custer's men affectionately called him, had little to do because Meade was not inclined to confront the Confederates. Stationed at Aquia Creek, Custer organized a band to keep up his men's spirits.

To replace the men who had been killed and wounded, the First Vermont Cavalry was temporarily attached to Custer's command. They were so enthusiastic about serving with Custer that they called themselves the Eighth Michigan, and like the men in the Michigan Brigade, they bedecked themselves with what had become the proud symbol of those who served under the "Boy General"—a red tie.

One day during this period of inactivity, Custer traveled the few miles south to Fredericksburg, Virginia. Although the Confederates occupied the town proper, the Fifth Michigan was headquartered at the Lacy House, on a high hill across the Rappahannock River from the city. Under a flag of truce, Custer crossed the river for a brief visit with some of his old West Point classmates, among them his good friend Tom Rosser, now a Confederate brigadier general.

Fredericksburg, Virginia; Rappahannock River in foreground

North of Culpeper, Virginia

September 13, 1863

At last, action came to the Michigan Brigade when the First, Second, and Third Cavalry Divisions marched on Jeb Stuart's headquarters in Culpeper, Virginia. The Union forces, numbering ten thousand men, formed a line five miles long. Custer's brigade, to the left in the line, was to attack a railroad train carrying Stuart's baggage and supplies. But the train pulled out before Custer reached it. He returned to find the rest of the Third Division under heavy fire from three of Stuart's batteries.

With the First Vermont, Custer charged the Rebels. In the charge, Custer's leg was wounded and his horse was killed. The Vermonters rolled on, capturing one gun and aiding in the capture of two more. Meanwhile, on a new mount, Custer led his men in a hell-for-leather charge into the town, forcing the Rebels to retreat. They fled so quickly that, at his headquarters, Stuart's uneaten dinner was left on the table.

September 14 to October 5, 1863

Because of his wound, Custer asked for fifteen days' leave, but Pleasonton, pleased with his actions in the last battle, rewarded him with twenty. Custer hurried home to Monroe, where he was lauded by the townspeople. Libbie urged him to ask her father for her hand, but the brave general, hero of many battles, could not summon the courage to face Judge Bacon. Libbie was adamant: There would be no engagement or even correspondence between them until her father approved. Custer promised to write the judge after he returned to Virginia.

October 10, 1863

Back with his brigade ten miles south of Culpeper, Custer learned the Third Division would be at the center of an advance on Stuart's cavalry, who were just across the nearby Rapidan River near its confluence with the Robertson River. The maneuver was part of a larger plan to reach Lee farther west.

Stuart attacked first, crossing the Robertson, and captured 250 men of the 106th New York Infantry. Ever ready, Custer dashed off with the Fifth Michigan and extricated most of the New Yorkers. As Kilpatrick arranged his forces on a hill overlooking the Confederates, Stuart sent a larger force over the Robertson. That night, the two sides watched each other warily, but neither made a move.

In the meantime, Lee had flanked Meade's infantry. Inexplicably, Meade removed his troops, leaving the cavalry to fend for itself.

Robertson River, south of Culpeper

October 11, 1863

After Meade abandoned the cavalry, Pleasonton ordered the Union forces to retreat across the Rappahannock. Custer and his Seventh Michigan formed the rear guard. As the Yankees moved out, Stuart moved in to flank them, and it looked as if he was about to cut off the entire division. Custer's brigade was surrounded.

Custer sent the Sixth Michigan to reinforce the Seventh in the rear, then aligned the First and Fifth Michigan into two columns with himself in front. Holding his saber aloft he said, "Boys of Michigan, there are some people between us and home; I'm going home. Who else goes?" The men roared their approval, the band struck up "Yankee Doodle," and, sabers glinting in the sun, they were off. They charged the Confederate line several times until finally it dissolved away.

The Union forces were so large, their retreat took many hours. It was 10 P.M. before the last of the division crossed the river.

Yet again, Custer was cited for bravery.

South of Culpeper

October 19, 1863

Instead of marching back to Washington, the cavalry was ordered to the vicinity of Warrenton, Virginia, where the enemy was thought to be lurking. Custer was in the vanguard when he found Stuart's troops at the Buckland grist mill on Broad Run, ten miles east of Warrenton. He sent the Seventh Michigan a mile downstream with orders to cross the creek and flank Stuart's troops. Upon hearing gunfire, Custer crossed the stream and forced the Confederates up a hill. Some of Custer's men routed Stuart's headquarters and forced him away, leaving another uneaten meal on the table.

Kilpatrick ordered Custer to move his men aside so the First Brigade could take the van; the Michiganders were to follow. But, feeling that his men had repulsed the Rebels too easily,

Custer sensed a trap. He reasoned that the Southerners were trying to make the Yankees rush in. To stall, he allowed his men to stop for dinner. Afterward, Custer sent the Sixth to explore the woods on his left flank. There they discovered Maj. Gen. Fitzhugh Lee with three brigades, waiting to cut them off.

The Sixth held Lee's men at bay until Custer brought reinforcements. He tried to hold open a passage for Kilpatrick but, pressed too hard, he had to withdraw. Custer's and Kilpatrick's men got away, but not without heavy casualties. Custer was chagrined to have been whipped by Fitzhugh Lee, one of his teachers at West Point. To make it worse, he learned that Tom Rosser's Laurel Brigade had been in the fight.

Broad Run, Buckland, Virginia

November 1863 to January 1864

As he had promised Libbie, Custer wrote to Judge Bacon and, in late November, he received the judge's consent to marry her. Now Autie and Libbie could correspond directly. Libbie wanted to wait a year before they married, but Custer wanted the wedding as soon as he could obtain leave. A series of impassioned, pleading letters from Custer finally persuaded her. In January, Custer received thirty days' leave and left with his staff for Monroe.

February 9, 1864

Elizabeth Clift Bacon and George Armstrong Custer were wed in the First Presbyterian Church of Monroe on February 9. The bride wore a magnificent gown of stiff white silk. Her long veil fell from a coronet of orange blossoms. The groom was resplendent in the regulation full-dress uniform of a brigadier general.

First Presbyterian Church, Monroe, Michigan

February 18, 1864

After the Custers' honeymoon, during which they visited Cleveland, New York, and Washington, they took up residence in Custer's headquarters at Clover Hill Farm in Stevensburg, Virginia, a few miles from Culpeper. It was unusual for officers' wives to accompany them to their commands, but Libbie, with her unassuming manner, quickly became popular with both the officers and the enlisted men.

Clover Hill Farm, Stevensburg, Virginia

February 28, 1864

Learning that Richmond was poorly defended, Kilpatrick wanted to attack the city with a strong force. He persuaded Pleasonton and Meade to let him carry out his plan, which was to send a decoy expedition into enemy territory to distract the Confederates from the real invasion to follow. Custer's Michigan Brigade was selected for the dangerous decoy mission. Since Libbie would not have adequate protection at Stevensburg, Custer sent her to Washington while he was gone.

In addition to diverting Rebel attention, Custer's brigade was to destroy the railroad bridge over the Rivanna River, just north of Charlottesville. As they moved south, they encountered pickets all along the way and captured a few prisoners. Within five miles of Charlottesville, the prisoners divulged that a large Confederate force occupied the city, so Custer went no farther. Before heading back to Stevensburg, however, he burned the railroad bridge as well as several mills. On the way back, the brigade narrowly escaped some of Stuart's troopers.

Kilpatrick's plan failed miserably. When he reached the outskirts of Richmond, a surprise Confederate attack caused heavy casualties before the Union leader fled.

Rivanna River, north of Charlottesville, Virginia

May 6 and 7, 1864

In March, Ulysses S. Grant, with the newly created rank of lieutenant general, assumed command of all Union armies. To his headquarters he brought Maj. Gen. Philip "Little Phil" Sheridan to replace Pleasonton as chief of cavalry. Custer's Michigan Brigade was elevated to the First Brigade and was transferred to the First Cavalry Division under Brig. Gen. Alfred Torbert. Kilpatrick was transferred to the West, and Brig. Gen. James H. Wilson took over the Third Division.

Knowing Lee's forces were badly supplied and Union troops outnumbered Rebels two to one, Grant decided to march on Richmond. On the night of May 5, Grant's army camped near The Wilderness—a desolate, dense thicket about fifteen miles west of Fredericksburg. At midnight, Custer was ordered to reinforce the Union's left flank at the crossroads of Brock Pike and Furnace Road. There, Custer deployed his men in the trees and scrub bordering an open field.

Just before sunrise, the Michiganders heard the high-pitched howl of the Rebel yell. A full brigade of Confederate cavalry chased Custer's pickets back to his main line. Custer ordered his troops forward, checking the enemy's advance momentarily. The Rebels brought up some artillery, but Custer's men held their position under the shelling and poured heavy fire from their Spencers into the gray line.

The Second Brigade arrived, and the combined forces drove the Confederates back. Ordered not to pursue, Custer turned his attention to destroying the nearby Catherine Furnace, a foundry for Confederate munitions.

Wilderness Battlefield at Brock Pike-Furnace Road intersection, Fredericksburg and Spotsylvania County National Military Park, near Fredericksburg, Virginia

May 9, 1864

Continuing the march to Richmond, Custer's brigade led Sheridan's column of ten thousand cavalry troopers. At Beaver Dam rail station, near the North Anna River, Custer's men captured two locomotives and one hundred freight cars loaded with supplies for the Rebels. They also set free nearly four hundred Union prisoners, who gladly joined Custer's force. After ransacking the trains, the Yankees torched everything in sight, including the station building. For good measure, Custer had his men rip up track on both sides of the station and tear down many miles of telegraph wires before they camped for the night.

Railroad tracks at Beaver Dam Station, Virginia

May 11, 1864

Realizing Sheridan was heading for Richmond, Stuart rode desperately for nine hours to get there ahead of him. At Yellow Tavern, on the northern outskirts of Richmond, Custer's brigade faced a line of Stuart's Invincibles stretching across the road. When the Southerners opened fire, Custer dismounted the Fifth and Sixth Michigan and ordered them to push the Rebels back. The Fifth was soon flanked. Dashing headlong through intense crossfire to get to them, Custer urged the men of the Fifth to hold on, and he stayed with them until the Sixth arrived.

Next, Custer led the First Regiment and the First Vermont in a charge against Stuart's battery. They made a magnificent spectacle as, in formation, they started their horses at a walk across the open field, re-forming in rows of three to cross a narrow bridge. When they came into range of the battery, which kept up a steady fire, they increased their pace to a trot. Then, as the bugle sounded the charge, the line of blue cut loose with a terrible yell and rode through the battery, capturing two guns and one hundred prisoners. Stuart was mortally wounded during Custer's charge and died the following day.

Yellow Tavern State Historic Site, Richmond, Virginia

May 28, 1864

Sheridan could not penetrate Richmond's outer defenses without the help of Meade's infantry, so he moved his troops to the southeast and let them rest for a few days. He then moved north to join Meade and Grant at Chesterland Station on the North Anna River. In the meantime, Brig. Gen. David McMurtrie Gregg's Second Cavalry Division struck the Confederate cavalry in their strong position behind log-and-rail breastworks at Haws Shop. The Second spent seven hours trying to drive the Rebels out, without success. By late afternoon the Yankees were in near panic from the fierce fighting and their frightful losses.

Custer and his Michigan Brigade were sent to the rescue. Arriving at dusk, Custer dismounted his men and lined them up on both sides of the road. Perfect targets as the only ones still mounted, Custer and his aide led a steady advance through the Second Division's line toward the Rebel fortifications. Encouraged, the men of the Second fell in behind Custer, and together they drove the Rebels from the field.

Haws Shop, near Studley, Virginia

June 11, 1864

Grant ordered Sheridan to move to the west to cut off Lee's supply lines to Richmond. Sheridan determined to do this with a quick raid, sending the First and Second Divisions to destroy the rail line at Trevilian Station. Lee got wind of Sheridan's intentions and sent the divisions of Fitzhugh Lee and Wade Hampton, who had replaced the fallen Stuart, to thwart the Yankees.

Using the First and Second Divisions to form his main line, Sheridan ordered Custer to slip around and flank the Rebels with his brigade. Custer's long line of troops proceeded slowly along a narrow road through dense woods. Those at the front came upon Hampton's undefended baggage train. Custer sent the Fifth Michigan under Col. Russell Alger to take the train. After doing so, Alger, overeager, spied the rear of Hampton's line beyond the railroad station and charged it.

A Rebel regiment cut off Alger, then advanced toward Custer, who was alone except for his staff and Pennington's battery; the rest of the brigade had not yet come up. When his four companies arrived, Custer dispatched them to cut through the gray line to Alger. After the rest of the brigade got there, Pennington's battery set up to rake the Confederates. But Tom Rosser's Laurel Brigade outflanked Custer. Just as Custer was ready to charge into Rosser's men, Fitzhugh Lee arrived on the scene and sealed off the Northerners' rear.

Surrounded and outnumbered, Custer formed his men into a circle around Pennington's battery for a stand. Dashing from place to place, he rallied his men, urging them on in a situation that was desperate and worsening by the minute. Realizing Custer was trapped, Sheridan ordered Alfred Torbert to go to his aid. Torbert's charge succeeded in saving Custer from one of the most harrowing predicaments of his life.

With Custer's casualties at 416, including 41 dead, 242 captured, and the rest wounded, this was the worst day of the war for the Wolverine brigade.

Site of Trevilian Station, near Trevilians, Virginia

~ Four ~

VICTORY
August 1864 to April 1865

August 9, 1864

Sheridan's forces, including Custer's Michigan Brigade, had been assigned to the Shenandoah Valley in Virginia, with nearby Harpers Ferry, West Virginia, as their base. Sheridan was to keep Confederate Lt. Gen. Jubal A. Early and his large command from invading Union territory, especially Washington, D.C. The Confederates knew that the threat of Early's presence in the valley would effectively draw Union forces away from Richmond. Early was also charged with protecting the harvest in what was called "the granary of the Confederacy"; Grant wanted Sheridan to destroy it.

Shenandoah Valley from Skyline Drive,
Shenandoah National Park, Virginia

Fire station, Harpers Ferry, West Virginia

August 16, 1864

Sheridan moved against the Confederates, but Early would not give him a fight and withdrew to the southwest. Custer, however, managed to engage some Rebels at Cedarville, along Crooked Run. He positioned his artillery opposite the Rebel guns on a high ridge overlooking the creek, with a clear shot to the west along the Winchester-Front Royal Pike. After both sides sniped at each other for the better part of an hour, the Graycoats charged across the creek, but the Union force repulsed them.

The Confederates next tried to outflank the Union line by crossing the creek a mile downstream. Custer moved two of his guns to a ridge above the ford and concealed the Fifth Michigan in a ravine behind the artillery. Thinking the Union guns were exposed and unsupported, the Confederates charged up the slope to take them—only to meet the full force of the Fifth, appearing seemingly out of nowhere. As Custer galloped across the front of the line, a bullet sheared away a lock of his hair.

Under the onslaught of the Wolverines' repeating Spencer carbines, the Rebels broke and ran pell-mell back to the ford. There, with reinforcements, they turned and managed to halt the Union advance. Then Custer summoned his own reinforcements, and when the reliable First Michigan arrived, the Confederates scattered. The Union took hundreds of prisoners. The fight lasted most of the day. Nearly forty Confederates had been killed; Custer lost eight men, with forty wounded.

Crooked Run, Cedarville, Virginia

August 25, 1864

Sheridan learned that Confederates under Fitzhugh Lee were again moving into Maryland, aiming to cross the Potomac at Williamsport. He sent Wilson's Third Cavalry Divisions and Torbert's First—including Custer's brigade—northwest from Harpers Ferry to check the Rebel advance. South of Shepardstown, West Virginia, Custer encountered two divisions of Southern infantry. Mistaking Custer's unit for a small patrol, the Rebels sent a regiment to run it off. Custer put up a successful defense, and the Rebel colonel was killed in the skirmish.

Soon afterward, Torbert realized he was vastly outnumbered and turned his division back toward Harpers Ferry, but the Rebel infantry pressured his rear guard and would not let him get away. Custer was ordered to drive the infantry back with his brigade. In doing so, the brigade became cut off from the rest of the division and found themselves with the Potomac at their back and Confederates in front and on either side. Custer, however, did not surrender. Arranging his men in a defensive horseshoe shape on the riverbank, he led them to a ford where they crossed the river to safety.

Potomac River at Shepardstown, West Virginia

September 19, 1864

In September, several divisions of Early's troops were called away from the Shenandoah Valley to protect Richmond. Sheridan, who had been criticized for sitting in Harpers Ferry and seemingly doing nothing, saw this as his opportunity to crush a weakened force. His plan was to cross Opequon Creek at several fords and move on Winchester, Virginia, putting Early on the defensive. Custer was to cross the creek at the northernmost crossing, Lockes Ford, with the Wolverines of his Seventh Michigan and the Twenty-fifth New York—the latter added to his brigade for this operation.

The Seventh and the Twenty-fifth assaulted a large force of Confederates in rifle pits across the creek, but failed to dislodge them. Custer sent in his old reliable First Michigan Regiment, encouraged by the band's rousing rendition of "Yankee Doodle." Slashing their way into the pits, the First displaced the Rebels, who retreated hastily toward Winchester ten miles south.

Custer fought his way toward the city in a series of skirmishes. In midafternoon, his brigade converged with the First and Second Divisions at the northern edge of town. There they found the whole Rebel cavalry positioned across the Winchester-Martinsburg Pike. The armies clashed with a terrible ferocity. Small groups of Union cavalry rushed full-tilt in every direction, attacking the Rebels wherever they could find them. The Northern charge rolled over the Southerners like an engulfing wave and washed them back past the infantry earthworks around Winchester.

To the southeast, Sheridan was pressing Early. Custer anticipated that Early would draw some of his men away from the Wolverine Brigade's vicinity. When he did, Custer took on the Confederate infantry, charging their earthworks so fiercely that whole companies threw down their arms and surrendered. His five hundred men took nearly eight hundred prisoners, along with two caissons and seven battle flags. Rarely had cavalry had such success against entrenched infantry.

Lockes Ford, Opequon Creek, Berryville, Virginia

October 9, 1864

At the end of September, Custer was given command of the Third Cavalry Division, who added red ties to their uniform as his old brigade had done. This meant he gave up the Michigan Brigade, which he had been leading for so long and had molded into a formidable fighting force. The tried-and-true Alexander Pennington, now a colonel, was also transferred to the Third to command a cavalry brigade. The First Vermont, however, returned to Custer's command.

In Virginia, Sheridan had advanced south past Harrisonburg in the Shenandoah Valley, but this made his supply and communications lines too long. He decided that withdrawal was his best course. On the march, he ordered his troops to seize all livestock and burn all crops and barns, but to spare the houses.

During the withdrawal, on October 9, Custer had a major engagement with his old friend Tom Rosser's Laurel Brigade at Toms Brook, halfway between Strasburg and Woodstock. Rosser's men had been bedeviling the Union rear guard for days. Now the Confederates took a strong position on the south side of the shallow brook, with their artillery on a high ridge above the stream, and dismounted cavalrymen behind stone fences beneath the ridge.

Dashing and chivalrous, Custer rode out alone in full view of the Rebels and their commander. He swept his hat from his head, bowed low from the saddle, and said, "Let's have a fair fight, boys! No malice!"

After scattered fire from both sides, Custer ordered three regiments move into position to charge the Southerners' left flank. Brig. Gen. Wesley Merritt's First Division was to charge the center; Custer and the Third would charge the right. As the Confederates skirmished with the First and Third, they heard a wild yelling and saw Custer's three flanking regiments advancing toward them. The Rebels turned and ran for two miles, until at last Rosser rallied them for a countercharge. Custer met Rosser's men in a grand charge that sent them fleeing ten miles up the valley.

After this battle, which came to be known as the "Woodstock Races," Tom Rosser's dress uniform was among the items the Yankees confiscated from his baggage. That night, Custer wrote a note to his friend. He thanked him for the gifts and asked him if, in the future, his tailor would kindly cut his coattails a little shorter to fit Custer better.

Toms Brook, near Woodstock, Virginia

October 16, 1864

By this time, Sheridan and his army had moved north down the valley to Middletown, where they established a camp on Cedar Creek. The Yankees intercepted a message revealing that the Confederates planned to attack the encampment shortly.

Cedar Creek Battlefield, Middletown, Virginia

October 19, 1864

The attack came a few days later, at four o'clock in the morning. Despite the advance warning, the Union was routed. Within an hour, Early had twenty-four Yankee guns in his possession. Most of the Union soldiers who had not been captured were fleeing toward Winchester, save one infantry division and the cavalry. Merritt's First Division and Custer's Third moved in to meet Early's twenty thousand infantrymen head-on. By this time it was late morning. Early's troops, certain in their victory, paused to plunder the abandoned Union camp. Because Early himself seemed in no hurry to press his obvious advantage, the severely outnumbered Union troops were able to hold him off.

By noon, Sheridan had arrived on the scene. Seeing most of his army in retreat, the general was furious. He galloped to and fro, urging the men back to the field. The presence of the popular general heartened the men. Sheridan marshaled his disarrayed troops, deploying the cavalry where it should have been—on the flanks. At about four o'clock he ordered a general advance.

When a gap opened in the Confederate line, Custer's Red Tie Boys thundered through it and ravaged the Rebels. Suddenly the Southerners were on the run, with Custer leading the pursuit.

Custer chased the Graycoats until dark. When he returned to Sheridan's headquarters at Belle Grove Plantation, the two generals danced together in jubilation around a huge bonfire. A near-disaster for the Union had turned into the beginning of the end for the Confederacy.

Custer was promoted to major general on October 25.

Belle Grove Plantation, Middletown, Virginia

November 1864

Sheridan's army was quartered in Winchester for the winter, and Libbie joined Custer at his winter headquarters at Long Meadow, the home of Mr. and Mrs. Robert Glass. Ever since their marriage, Custer had missed no opportunity to be with Libbie.

Custer's younger brother, Lt. Thomas Ward Custer, had enlisted at age sixteen, and had served with distinction in the war's western theater. Now, three years later, Tom joined his brother's staff. In public, Custer maintained a rigid formality with Tom, even piling extra duties on him to avoid any suggestion of favoritism, but in the privacy of their home, the two roughhoused like schoolboys.

Long Meadow, Winchester, Virginia

December 19, 1864

The First and Second Divisions were sent south to Charlottesville to cut the rail line supplying Lee, while Custer's Third Division moved south up the Shenandoah Valley to distract the Confederates. After marching seventy-five miles through bitter cold and deep snow, Custer's men camped at Lacey Spring. Knowing his presence had been detected and thus expecting an attack, Custer roused his troops at four o'clock in the morning so they would not be surprised.

Indeed, Tom Rosser attacked at 5 A.M. Some of his troops surrounded the house where Custer himself was still asleep. When Custer awoke and saw the Graycoats, he put on the coat he had captured from Rosser, coolly walked out the door, mounted his horse, and rode through the Rebels to join his troops.

The First Vermont drove the Confederates back a mile. Both sides took prisoners and incurred losses. Rosser did not press Custer further, and rather than prolong his men's exposure to the debilitating cold, Custer returned to Winchester.

Lacey Spring, Virginia

March 2, 1865

By January, it was evident that Early had insufficient troops to be a threat to Union forces in the Shenandoah Valley. Nevertheless, when Early found out the Federals were headed south, he planned to make a stand at Waynesboro. On March 2, Custer and his men, the first to arrive in the town, discovered what was left of Early's army—two brigades of infantry, a considerable number of artillery pieces, and the severely depleted ranks of Rosser's Laurel Brigade—in good defensive positions. The infantrymen were in trenches overlooking an open field; the artillery was positioned to cover the main road. But Custer saw immediately that Early had overlooked something important: His left flank was unsupported. The Confederate leader did not use the South River as a natural defense; instead, he placed his left flank some distance away from the river.

Custer acted quickly, before the Confederates had a chance to figure out his tactics. Without waiting for the rest of the army, he sent troops through the woods to flank Early's left, placed his artillery to sweep the Rebel line, and readied his remaining two brigades for a charge.

Thus deployed, Custer's units all went into action at once. As the frontal charge collapsed the Rebel line and rolled on to the battery, the flankers swept to the rear, cutting off the only escape route. In just three hours, it was all over for the Confederates.

The Red Tie Boys captured 1,400 prisoners, 17 battle flags, and 11 guns. Early, his staff, and Rosser escaped.

South River, Riverside Park, Waynesboro, Virginia

The Farm, Charlottesville, Virginia

March 3, 1865

With the Shenandoah Valley now cleared of Confederates, Sheridan jubilantly led his army over the Blue Ridge Mountains to assist Grant in the siege of Richmond. At Charlottesville, the army halted for a few days. Just outside the city, the mayor met Custer and surrendered the keys to the public buildings to prevent their destruction. At one point during his stay, Custer had his headquarters at The Farm, a house in the city.

March 31, 1865

For more than nine months, Lee and his Army of Northern Virginia had been holed up behind defenses in Petersburg, Virginia, south of Richmond. Grant was concerned that, if attacked, Lee's men might escape and join Confederate forces in North Carolina, prolonging the war. Sheridan was resting his troops and replenishing his supplies at White House Landing on the York River when Grant ordered him to move around Lee's right flank at Petersburg to prevent escape, and also to cut off the Danville and Southside Railroads. Lee found out about the plan and dispatched his cavalry, along with five infantry brigades under Maj. Gen. George E. Pickett, to quash it.

In a fight at Dinwiddie Courthouse on March 31, Custer held Pickett's men back. Pickett withdrew to Five Forks, a key crossroads about fifteen miles southwest of Petersburg. There he established a line of earthworks nearly a mile long.

April 1, 1865

Sheridan moved his forces to Five Forks. There Custer, on the left side of the Union line, ordered two brigades to flank the enemy's unsupported right. Meanwhile, the rest of his command attacked the Rebel breastworks. The maneuver worked. Custer and his men galloped over the fortifications, pushing the Rebels back to the swamp at Hatchers Run, while Sheridan and his troops demolished the rest of the Confederate line. The Yankees severed the Southern rail lines and took five thousand prisoners, decimating an entire wing of Lee's army.

Hatchers Run, north of Dinwiddie, Virginia

April 3, 1865

After the action at Five Forks, Lee evacuated his entire force from Petersburg and Richmond and began a race to get around Sheridan's army and reach North Carolina. Custer rushed ahead to help stop the escape. In a running battle at Namozine Church, Custer's men drove two Confederate divisions back to the rear of their line.

Namozine Church, Amelia County, Virginia

Saylers Creek Battlefield State Historical Park near Rice, Virginia

April 6, 1865

Avoiding the Northern army, Lee moved northwest as Sheridan moved west. Custer received word that Lee's hastily assembled baggage train of wagons was headed for the ford at Saylers Creek, an hour's ride away. The Second Division encountered the Confederates first, but the Rebels managed to repulse their attack. When Custer arrived he spotted a gap in the Rebel line and charged his men through it. The Third captured a battery and eight hundred prisoners, and destroyed three hundred wagons in the train.

Two Rebel divisions went after Custer and drove him away from the train. Quickly

Saylers Creek Battlefield

reforming, Custer's men, under heavy fire, charged some hastily built Rebel defenses. After repeated charges, Union reinforcements from the Sixth Infantry Corps arrived, and the Yanks were finally able to overrun the enemy line. The Union took thousands of prisoners, six generals among them.

Richmond–Lynchburg stage road, Appomattox Court House National Historical Park, Appomattox, Virginia

April 9, 1865

During the night of April 8, Custer's division captured four of Lee's railroad supply trains at Appomattox Station, east of Lynchburg, Virginia. By the next morning, Union forces had Lee's men pinned down near Appomattox Court House. Custer's Third was deployed across the Lynchburg Pike to prevent the Rebels from escaping. The Third held their ground through several skirmishes during the morning, until infantry reinforcements arrived.

McLean House, Appomattox Court House National Historical Park

Custer was organizing his men for a charge when an aide of Lt. Gen. James Longstreet rode in with a flag of truce and requested a cessation of hostilities. Later that afternoon, Lee met with Grant at the McLean House in Appomattox, where they drew up terms of surrender.

Now that the fighting was over, Custer sought out his Confederate West Point class-mates for a joyous reunion.

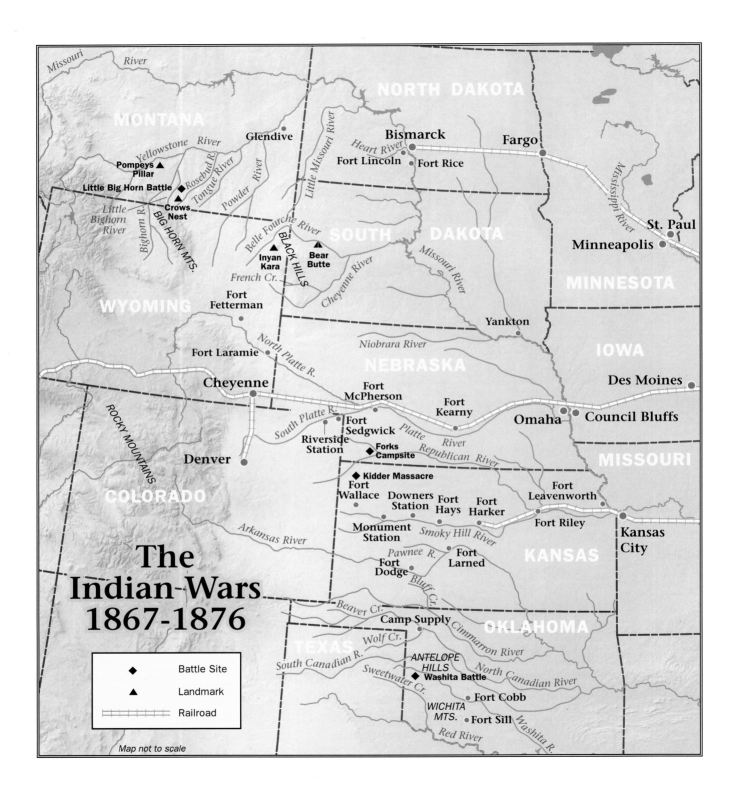

The Indian Wars 1867-1876

Missouri River

MONTANA

NORTH DAKOTA

Glendive

Bismarck

Fargo

Yellowstone River

Heart River

Pompeys Pillar ▲

Fort Lincoln

Fort Rice

Rosebud R.

Little Big Horn Battle ◆

Tongue River

Powder River

Little Missouri River

Crows Nest ▲

Bighorn R.

Little Bighorn River

BIG HORN MTS.

Belle Fourche River

St. Paul

BLACK HILLS

SOUTH DAKOTA

Minneapolis

Inyan Kara ▲

Bear Butte ▲

French Cr.

Cheyenne River

Missouri River

MINNESOTA

WYOMING

Fort Fetterman

Yankton

Niobrara River

IOWA

Fort Laramie

North Platte R.

NEBRASKA

Des Moines

Cheyenne

Fort McPherson

Fort Kearny

Omaha

Council Bluffs

South Platte R.

Fort Sedgwick

Platte River

Riverside Station

Republican River

MISSOURI

Denver

◆ Forks Campsite

◆ Kidder Massacre

Fort Wallace

Downers Station

Fort Hays

Fort Harker

Fort Leavenworth

COLORADO

Monument Station

Smoky Hill River

Fort Riley

Kansas City

Arkansas River

Pawnee R.

Fort Larned

KANSAS

Fort Dodge

Bluff Cr.

The Indian Wars 1867-1876

Beaver Cr.

Camp Supply

OKLAHOMA

TEXAS

Wolf Cr.

Cimmarron River

South Canadian R.

Sweetwater Cr.

ANTELOPE HILLS

◆ Washita Battle

North Canadian River

WICHITA MTS.

Fort Cobb

Fort Sill

Washita R.

Red River

Rocky Mountains

◆ Battle Site

▲ Landmark

╫╫╫ Railroad

Map not to scale

⫷ Five ⫸

HEADING WEST
June 1865 to October 1867

June 18, 1865

Custer, now twenty-five, assumed command of the Cavalry Division of the Military District of the Southwest in Alexandria, Louisiana.

The Civil War was officially over, but factions of Confederates moved into Mexico, where Emperor Maximilian, building an army, welcomed

Ruins of Sherman Institute, Alexandria, Louisiana

them for their military expertise. Ulysses Grant, who remained the army's commanding general until his inauguration as president in 1869, wanted the Texas border protected from insurgents and selected Custer for the job.

Libbie accompanied her husband to Alexandria. Often in the evening they would ride out to the grounds of the Sherman Institute, named for William Tecumseh Sherman, who had been its principal before the war. The Union hero Sherman was now commander of the Division of the Missouri.

In addition to Custer's duties as military governor, he had to whip his new command into shape. The days of enthusiastic and adoring Red Tie Boys were over. Now, Custer's troops consisted mainly of discontented soldiers serving out their enlistments. To mold them into a strong fighting unit, Custer often had to impose harsh discipline.

November 23, 1865

His command trained, Custer marched them to Austin, Texas, where the governor offered the general the vacant Blind Asylum building for his headquarters. Custer was popular in Austin; his presence ensured that law and order would prevail during the unsettled months after the war.

Austin was famous for its horse racing, so in his free time, Custer was able to participate in one of his favorite sports. Custer also often took Libbie and his staff to the top of Mt. Bonnell for picnics, serenaded by the army band.

Mount Bonnell, Austin, Texas

Former Blind Asylum building, on campus of University of Texas, Austin

January-September 1866

After a little over two months in Texas, Custer was ordered to move his troops east to join the Fifth Cavalry. His wartime rank of brevet major general was reduced to captain. Upon his return from Texas, Custer considered retiring from the army and for many months fruitlessly searched for suitable employment. He even applied for a commission as a lieutenant general in the Mexican Republican Army, which was trying to overthrow Maximilian, but the U.S. Army would not grant him a leave of absence. In Michigan, enthusiastic supporters urged him to run for senator or governor, but Custer had no desire to enter politics.

Ultimately, conditions in the West determined Custer's employment. With the Union Pacific and Kansas Pacific Railroads stretching into Indian territory, bringing immigrants by the thousands onto Indian lands, Indian depredations were on the rise.

In response to the Indian crisis, the army formed four new cavalry regiments. In July, Custer accepted a commission as a lieutenant colonel in the Seventh Cavalry. The regiment's official commander was Col. A. J. Smith, but Smith had other duties as commander of the District of Upper Arkansas, so Custer served as acting commander.

October 20, 1866

Custer reported to his new regiment at Fort Riley, Kansas. His troops were a motley group. The majority of the enlisted men were new recruits, including some recently arrived immigrants. Most were uneducated and poor, and had joined the army hoping for a better life. As for Custer's officers, some were Civil War veterans, but others were unseasoned and had little leadership ability. In addition, Custer had to deal with jealousy and drunkenness among his officers—the latter was a major problem.

Custer house, Fort Riley, Junction City, Kansas

April 7-12, 1867

Maj. Gen. Winfield Scott Hancock, with whom Custer had briefly fought in the Civil War, joined the Seventh Cavalry at Fort Riley. Hancock was to command an expedition to clear the Indians from the land between the Arkansas and Platte Rivers. Lieutenant General Sherman had instructed Hancock to give the Indians "no quarter," and Hancock vowed to take "no insolence . . . from any band." Hancock, Custer, and their troops marched over 150 miles to Fort Larned, Kansas, where Hancock established his headquarters. He had sent word that he wanted to hold a council with the Cheyennes and Sioux there on April 10. Hancock claimed he wanted peace with the Indians, but they were apprehensive about dealing with whites, especially after soldiers massacred five hundred of their people at Sand Creek, in southern Colorado Territory, in November 1864.

A snowstorm on April 9 provided the Indians with an excuse not to come in to Fort Larned, but a few days later two chiefs arrived to parley. Hancock sternly warned them against killing white settlers and taking white women captive. He told them he wanted to go to their village and meet with the rest of the chiefs.

Fort Larned, Larned, Kansas

April 13 and 14, 1867

The Sioux and Cheyenne village was about thirty miles west of Fort Larned on Pawnee Fork. The Indians believed the soldiers were coming to destroy them. Some distance from the village, warriors lined up across the soldiers' path, and Hancock deployed his men into battle formation. After some tense moments, the chiefs agreed to parley with Hancock that night in his camp, about half a mile from the village.

When the chiefs, including Roman Nose, a Cheyenne, and Pawnee Killer, a Sioux, arrived, they told Hancock that their women and children had fled in fear of another incident like the one at Sand Creek. Hancock reassured the chiefs and told them it was safe to bring back those who had run away. The chiefs agreed to do so. That night, at Hancock's direction, Custer and his men surrounded the village to prevent the Indians from escaping. But when Custer and two others crept into the village, they found it deserted.

Pawnee Fork, west of Larned, Kansas

April 15, 1867

Furious at the Indians' sudden departure, Hancock sent Custer and the Seventh in pursuit. The Indians' trail headed north. Distinct at first, after several miles the trail became too broken and faint to follow.

April 16 and 17, 1867

Custer continued north to the Smoky Hill River to warn stationkeepers along the stage route there to prepare for Indian hostilities. When Custer reached Downers Station, it was deserted. He discovered that station employees were holed up together in every fourth station for a stronger defense. Proceeding east, Custer found that Indians had burned the deserted stations. But not all inhabitants had had time to leave. In the still-smoking ashes of Lookout Station, fifteen miles west of Fort Hays, Kansas, Custer found the mutilated bodies of three white men.

When Hancock heard of the murders, he ordered the abandoned Indian village burned, increasing the Indians' animosity.

Downers Station site, west of Trego City, Kansas

Big Creek, south of Victoria, Kansas

May 1867

Low on supplies, Custer returned to Fort Hays. Libbie joined him there shortly afterward. As soon as they had set up their camp on a small rise on Big Creek, Custer resumed his search for the Indians.

Western Kansas

June 1, 1867

Custer and the Seventh Cavalry set out on June 1 for a thousand-mile scout of the country. From Fort Hays, they would march north to Fort McPherson on the Platte River in Nebraska, then swing southwest to the forks of the Republican River, northwest to the Platte again near Fort Sedgwick, in Colorado Territory, and finally south to Fort Wallace, Kansas, on the Smoky Hill River.

June 10-18, 1867

At his camp on the Jack Morrow ranch, twelve miles from Fort McPherson, Custer met with the Sioux leader Pawnee Killer and several other chiefs. The Indians hoped to learn Custer's plans at the council. Custer requested that they move their village closer to the fort so the army could keep a closer watch on them. The Indians intimated that they would.

On June 15, General Sherman, who made no secret of his hatred of Indians, arrived at Fort McPherson. Sure that Pawnee Killer had no intention of honoring Custer's request, he sent Custer to confront the chief and any other Indians camped at the forks of the Republican. Custer took the quickest and easiest route to the village, through Morrows Canyon.

Morrows Canyon, southeast of North Platte, Nebraska

June 21-28, 1867

At the forks of the Republican, Custer set up camp, planning to stay for several days. He sent a detail to Fort Sedgwick to send and receive dispatches and a wagon train to Fort Wallace to get supplies. He also sent word to Libbie, whom he believed had left Fort Hays and was waiting to meet him at Fort Wallace, to come to his camp with the supply train.

At daybreak on June 24, a picket discovered hundreds of Indians advancing on the camp and fired a shot to wake the sleeping troopers. Under heavy fire, the warriors withdrew about a mile. Custer sent an interpreter to arrange a parley at the river, midway between the two groups. Custer specified that six people should represent each side.

Six chiefs, led by Pawnee Killer, came to meet Custer. As they talked, armed warriors emerged from the tall grass on the far side of the river and began to cross over. Custer warned Pawnee Killer that if any more warriors crossed the river, he would order his full command to advance. The chief signaled his remaining warriors to stay where they were.

Custer repeated his request that Pawnee Killer move his village closer to the fort as a show of friendship, but the chief refused.

At a stalemate, the Indians galloped back across the river toward their village. Custer and his men rode in pursuit, but the heavy army horses could not keep up with the fleet Indian ponies. After several hours, the soldiers abandoned the chase.

June 29, 1867

Custer's detail returned from Fort Sedgwick with orders for Custer to find some Indians who had been seen near Riverside Station on the South Platte River. The next day, the wagon train from Fort Wallace arrived. Libbie was not with it because she had not been at Fort Wallace. This turned out to be fortunate, since Indians attacked the wagons on the way back, resulting in a running fight that lasted three hours.

South of Benkelman, Nebraska

July 5-7, 1867

When Custer arrived at Riverside Station on July 5, having sighted no Indians, he received word that a detachment under 2d Lt. Lyman S. Kidder had been sent out with new orders for him several days before, but Kidder's party had not been heard from since.

Custer prepared to march to Fort Wallace the next morning. During the night, thirty-five of Custer's men deserted. Riverside Station was on the main route to Denver and the Colorado gold and silver fields, so for men who had no intention of serving out their enlistments if a better opportunity presented itself, it was a good place to depart. On the next day's march, thirteen more men tried to desert during the noon break, in full view of the regiment.

Custer knew he had to act swiftly and severely with the deserters. To curb the growing problem of desertion, General Sheridan had directed his officers to shoot deserters without trial if deemed necessary. Accordingly, Custer dispatched several officers to bring back the deserters. Seven deserters who were on horseback got away, but the other six, afoot, were captured. Three of these were shot and wounded while resisting capture. Custer took the deserters back to Fort Wallace.

Riverside Station site on South Platte River, west of Crook, Colorado

July 11, 1867

Continuing to Fort Wallace, Custer came upon the bodies of Kidder and his men. It appeared that they had died in a running fight with Indians. The bodies were badly mutilated, and some of them showed evidence of torture. After pausing to bury the bodies, Custer continued on with his men.

Kidder Massacre site, south of Bird City, Kansas

July 13, 1867

Custer expected Libbie to have arrived at Fort Wallace by the time he got there, but she had not. Having no idea where she was, he became terribly concerned for her safety. In addition to raiding Indians, an epidemic of cholera was raging in Kansas along the Smoky Hill River stage route and at most of the forts. Custer found Fort Wallace in deplorable condition. Cholera and two recent Indian attacks had decimated the ranks. The food was unfit for consumption, and medical supplies were scarce.

General Hancock, who was supposed to have met Custer at Fort Wallace, had moved himself to the more comfortable Fort Leavenworth. Custer was to have received new orders from Hancock. Even more frustrating, the provisions that were supposed to be waiting there were nowhere to be found. Inadequate supplies were a continuing problem, and Custer had repeatedly complained to Hancock about his provisions. When he received them at all, they were usually of such poor quality that they were unusable.

Fort Wallace site, southeast of Wallace, Kansas

Monument Rocks, Gove County, Kansas

July 15 and 16, 1867

Having found neither Hancock nor his orders at Fort Wallace, and with his command in desperate need of supplies, Custer decided to move on to Seventh Cavalry headquarters at Fort Harker, Kansas, about two hundred miles east. He took seventy-two of his healthiest men and whatever horses were serviceable. The next day, riding along the Smoky Hill stage route, the contingent stopped to eat and rest for several hours at Monument Station.

Castle Rock, Gove County, Kansas

July 17, 1867

Just past Castle Rock Station, one of the troopers' horses played out. Custer, in the advance, sent a seven-man detail back with a fresh mount. As the party returned to the column, they were attacked by Indians, who killed one trooper and wounded another. At Downers Station, Custer sent a squad of infantry, now stationed there, to bury the dead man and bring in the wounded one, while Custer's party pressed on.

Fort Harker, Kanopolis, Kansas

July 18, 1867

Upon reaching Big Creek stage station, sixty miles from Fort Harker, Custer sent his men the short distance north to Fort Hays to rest for a day and to obtain an ambulance and mules to replace their tired horses. Custer knew Libbie was not at Fort Hays; he had learned that a flood in early June had wiped out their camp on Big Creek, and all the women at the fort had been sent to Fort Riley. There was a chance that Libbie had since gone to Fort Harker, so Custer was impatient to get there. He continued on, accompanied only by his brother Tom and three other men.

July 19, 1867

Custer arrived at Fort Harker at 2 A.M. and awakened the commander, Col. A. J. Smith. Custer related the details of his expedition to Smith, including what had happened to Kidder and the miserable situation at Fort Wallace.

Libbie, it turned out, was not at Fort Harker. Custer, assuming she was still at Fort Riley, requested and received permission from Colonel Smith to go there, and he departed on the next train.

July 21, 1867

Libbie was indeed safe at Fort Riley, and she returned with her husband to Fort Harker. Upon their arrival, however, the Custers received a shock. On orders from Hancock, Smith had Custer placed under arrest. Among the charges were leaving Fort Wallace without permission, abandoning his soldiers at Downers Station, marching his men excessively, procuring an ambulance and four mules at Fort Hays for his personal use, and excessive cruelty and illegal conduct in shooting the three deserters.

As Libbie was with Custer, Smith sent them both back to the greater comfort of Fort Riley to await the court-martial.

September 15 to October 11, 1867

Custer's court-martial took place at Fort Leavenworth. He pleaded not guilty to all charges. He had hoped to have Sherman testify on his behalf, but the general was not available. In fact, most of the officers Custer wanted as witnesses for his defense were unavailable—the army had determined it "inconvenient" for them to leave their posts. The verdict was guilty on all counts. Custer's sentence—mild for the charges—was suspension of rank and pay for one year.

Custer believed he would never have been tried at all if Hancock had not wanted to divert attention from his own sorry record in the recent Indian campaigns. Furthermore, Custer maintained that his trial violated the Seventy-fifth Article of War because some members of the panel were junior in rank to his, and three of them, all in fact on Hancock's staff, had never had a command of their own. One of these was the commissary officer who had been directly responsible for a good share of Custer's supply problems. Sheridan told Custer he would try to have the sentence remitted, but Custer firmly refused the offer.

~ Six ~

UNREST IN KANSAS
Winter 1867-68 to March 1873

Winter 1867-68 to Summer 1868

In the fall of 1867, General Sheridan was given command of the Department of the Missouri and Hancock was shunted off to a command in New Orleans. Sheridan planned to take up residence at Fort Leavenworth the following spring. In the meantime, he offered the Custers the use of his house, which they gratefully accepted. The couple spent a quiet winter there, and in the spring, they went to Monroe for a lengthy visit.

Officer's residence, Fort Leavenworth, Leavenworth, Kansas

October 7, 1868

During the summer, Indians from various tribes had murdered over 150 whites, taken nearly 30 women and children captive, and committed numerous other depredations. In October Sheridan, after waging a series of unsuccessful actions against the Indians, summoned Custer back to duty to lead a winter campaign.

Custer joined his regiment at its camp on Bluff Creek, southeast of Fort Dodge, Kansas. Just after he assumed command, a small group of Indians attacked the encampment. It was a decoy party trying to lure the troops out. Since this sort of maneuver had been almost a daily occurrence, the soldiers did not fall for the trick.

Bluff Creek vicinity, south of Bucklin, Kansas

November 12-18, 1868

After spending most of October training his troops—several hundred of whom were new recruits—Custer marched south toward Indian territory with the Seventh Cavalry. At the fork of Wolf and Beaver Creeks, about midway between the Cimarron and Canadian Rivers, Custer established a base of operations called Camp Supply. Sheridan joined him there shortly, with the Nineteenth Kansas Volunteer Cavalry.

Beaver Creek, Fort Supply, Oklahoma

Antelope Hills, near Canadian River, north of Roll, Oklahoma

November 23-26, 1868

Hoping to make a swift strike against the rampaging Indians, Custer started south with only his own regiment. Heavy snow forced him to navigate by compass.

On the morning of November 26, at the crossing of the Canadian River near the Antelope Hills, a scouting detachment found the fresh trail of an estimated 150 warriors. Custer tracked the Indians through snow now eighteen inches deep.

The column halted for the night behind a ridge. After scouts reported smelling smoke,

Bluffs north of Washita battle site, near Cheyenne, Oklahoma

Custer went to the crest of the ridge. There he heard dogs barking and a baby crying, indicating the Indian encampment was somewhere below him on the Washita River. He decided to attack at dawn.

November 27, 1868

The soldiers easily overran the unsuspecting Indians. Though Custer told his men to spare the women and children as much as possible, the troops killed fifteen women and nine children in the battle, two deliberately. One was a boy who had tried to gun down an officer at close range, and the other was an Indian woman who, rather than surrender a captive white boy, slit open his stomach.

Custer lost one man in the engagement and fourteen were wounded. In addition, a detachment of nineteen men under Maj. Joel H. Elliott was missing. The Indians later reported that, along with the women and children killed, they lost thirteen men, though Custer's official report listed 103 warriors killed. The soldiers also captured fifty-three women and children. The Indians' pony herd was too large to take back to Camp Supply, so Custer ordered most of the animals shot.

Custer learned from some of the captives that the village, one of several along the river, had been that of Black Kettle, a peaceful Cheyenne who had been killed in the fight. He also learned that the Indians he had trailed to the village had just returned from raids on white settlements. As was often the case, a peaceful chief could not prevent his young warriors from raiding.

As Custer prepared for the march back to Camp Supply, he noticed a large number of warriors gathered on the bluffs around the camp. Concerned about a possible attack, he and his troops rode toward the other villages along the Washita, hoping the Indians would think they were going to attack them. The ruse worked. As soon as the Indians withdrew, Custer departed.

Site of Cheyenne village, Washita River, near Cheyenne, Oklahoma

December 1868

After a few days at Camp Supply, Custer, Sheridan, and the Nineteenth Kansas set off toward Fort Cobb, farther south on the Washita, where Sheridan would establish his headquarters. On the way, the party searched for Elliott's detachment. About two miles from the site of Black Kettle's village, they found all twenty men dead, their bodies mutilated.

Some days after Custer and Sheridan resumed the march, a group of Kiowas approached waving a white flag. The two officers met with a delegation of about twenty chiefs, including Lone Wolf and Satanta. To prove they were friendly, the chiefs agreed to accompany Sheridan and Custer to Fort Cobb and to send messengers to their people telling them to meet them there. But during the day and that night, the chiefs slipped away one by one, until only Lone Wolf and Satanta remained. Sensing trickery, Sheridan ordered Lone Wolf and Satanta held as hostages until they reached the fort.

When the Kiowas failed to arrive at Fort Cobb after several days, Sheridan sent word to the village saying they had until sundown the next day to show up, or the two chiefs would be hung. The ploy worked, and the tribe moved to the reservation at the fort.

Fort Cobb, Oklahoma

January 1869

Although the Kiowas had been subdued, a band of Cheyennes and a band of Arapahos were still at large. On January 14, Custer and forty men, with a Cheyenne and an Arapaho chief as guides, set out southwest in pursuit of the bands. In the Quartz Mountains, the party sent smoke signals from a high peak to announce their arrival to a nearby village. Custer found the Arapaho encampment just beyond the mountains, and after a peaceful parley with the chiefs, he persuaded the Indians to move to the reservation.

Quartz (Wichita) Mountains, south of Lone Wolf, Oklahoma

February 1869

Running short of supplies, Custer could not go after the Cheyennes, who were reported to be in Texas. With the Arapahos in tow, he headed for Fort Sill, where a new reservation had been constructed adjacent to a holy place the Indians called Medicine Bluff.

Medicine Bluff, Fort Sill, Lawton, Oklahoma

March 2-14, 1869

After reprovisioning at Fort Sill, Custer and his full regiment left to find the Cheyenne village. He followed the Wichita Mountains to the west until he found an Indian campsite that was not more than two weeks old. From there, he followed tracks north.

Wichita Mountains west of Lawton, Oklahoma

March 15, 1869

Custer found the Cheyenne village on Sweetwater Creek, just west of the Texas border. He had information that two white women were being held there. Without mentioning the captives, Custer asked the Cheyenne chiefs to come to the reservation. Although the chiefs smoked the peace pipe with Custer, they had no intention of returning to the reservation and planned to flee at the first opportunity.

Learning this, Custer took four Cheyenne hostages. He sent the chiefs a message saying he would release the hostages, as well as the women and children he had captured during the fight at the Washita, when the Cheyennes returned the white women and went to the reservation.

For four days, the Cheyennes stalled. Finally, Custer gave them a deadline, after which, he let them know, the hostages would be hung. Just before the deadline, the Indians surrendered the two captive women and started for Fort Sill. Custer took the three hostages to Fort Hays, where they were housed in separate quarters but in the same stockade as the Cheyenne captives.

Sweetwater Creek vicinity, east of Wheeler, Texas

April and May 1869

Custer escorted Libbie from Fort Leavenworth to his camp near Fort Hays. The Seventh Cavalry was again encamped on Big Creek, but in a location less prone to flooding. The Custers' living quarters consisted of four tents that served as a sitting room, a bedroom, a dining room, and a guest room.

The Cheyenne hostages Custer had brought in had been acting suspiciously, so they were moved from the stockade to the guardhouse. During the move, they pulled out knives. In the ensuing struggle, one army sergeant and two hostages were killed. About a month later, the captives were released and transported to the reservation at Fort Sill.

Custer campsite, Fort Hays Experiment Station, Hays, Kansas

Buffalo

Summer 1869

Sheridan had promised Custer that after Col. A. J. Smith retired as commander of the Seventh Cavalry, he would try to secure the position for Custer. Nevertheless, Custer lost out to Col. Samuel Sturgis.

Some of the Cheyennes had left the reservation and returned to their nomadic ways, but they caused few disturbances, and Custer was bored with the inactivity. To keep himself occupied, Custer organized buffalo hunts. By summer's end, more than two hundred people, including two English lords, had participated in the hunts.

Custer and Libbie spent much of the winter at Fort Leavenworth.

May 1870 to August 1871

In May, Custer and Libbie returned to Fort Hays. Although Indian activity had increased in the area, army patrols brought in only a few Indians; most had moved north into Nebraska.

Early in 1871, Custer learned that the Seventh Cavalry was to be broken up and stationed all over the country. Custer asked for an extended leave to seek civilian work. He spent five months looking for a job in New York and Monroe, to no avail.

Horse farm, Louisville, Kentucky

September 1871 to March 1873

Returning to active duty, Custer was assigned to take two companies of the reorganized Seventh Cavalry to Elizabethtown, Kentucky, to subdue bootleggers and the newly organized Ku Klux Klan. During their two and a half years in "Betseytown," the Custers boarded at Hill House. Custer often went to area breeders to purchase horses for the army. He also began writing a series of articles about his experiences on the plains for *Galaxy* magazine.

Former Hill House, now Brown–Pusey House, Elizabethtown, Kentucky

Fort Rice State Historic Site, Fort Rice, South Dakota

— Seven —

THE BLACK HILLS
March 1873 to May 1876

Spring 1873

In March, Custer was ordered to reassemble the Seventh Cavalry in Memphis, Tennessee, and proceed to Yankton, Dakota Territory, where the Sioux were causing trouble. From Yankton, the troops marched five hundred miles upriver to Fort Rice. Ten days after arriving at the fort, the men of the Seventh were sent out to protect Northern Pacific Railroad surveyers from Indian attack along the Yellowstone River. Custer was delighted to find that the chief engineer of the project was his friend, former classmate, and worthy adversary during the Civil War, Tom Rosser.

August 4, 1873

The Treaty of 1868 between the government and the Sioux permitted the construction of railroads in lands north of the North Platte River and east of the Bighorn Mountains. But the Indians did not understand the provisions of the treaty, and believed the survey crew and its military escort were violating it.

Around noon Custer and eighty-five men, out ahead of the main column, stopped for a break on the Yellowstone River near the mouth of the Tongue. While there they spotted six Sioux warriors near the army horse herd. Custer realized immediately that they were decoys trying to lure the troops out to a much larger force of warriors who lay in wait.

Custer had a ruse of his own. He and his orderly rode out ahead of the detail to provoke the Indians to attack. The Sioux took the bait, and the two led three hundred warriors back to the waiting soldiers, who managed to hold them off with their Spencers until the rest of the command came up. With the reinforcement, the troopers quickly routed the Sioux.

West of Miles City, Montana

August 8-11, 1873

Custer's scouts discovered the trail of a large Sioux village moving west along the Yellowstone River. Following the trail, Custer and his men found that, two miles from the mouth of the Bighorn River, the Sioux had crossed the Yellowstone in bull boats. The soldiers attempted to cross, but their horses balked at the river's swift current. Custer decided to camp overnight on the shore.

The next day, eight hundred Indians commenced firing at the troopers from across the river. After several hours of futile bombardment, three hundred warriors recrossed the Yellowstone, both downstream and upstream of Custer's camp, and tried to take the bluff behind the camp. Custer ordered a mounted charge. The cavalrymen drove off the Indians and chased them for eight miles.

August 15, 1873

As the railroad surveyors finished their work and prepared to leave, the Sioux attacked one last time. The troops were camped on the north side of the Yellowstone, opposite a large sandstone formation known as Pompeys Pillar. Some of the men were in the water, seeking relief from the brutal August heat, when Indians fired on them from across the river. The soldiers returned fire, and the Indians left.

Pompeys Pillar National Monument, Pompeys Pillar, Montana

Missouri River, Fort Abraham Lincoln, Mandan, North Dakota

September 21, 1873

With the railroad expedition completed, the Seventh Cavalry moved to Fort Abraham Lincoln, five miles south of Mandan in Dakota Territory. Fort Abraham Lincoln was the first post under Custer's direct command. It stood atop a broad, flat bluff that rose abruptly from the Missouri River. Low hills formed a perimeter to the west. The officers' quarters, in a row in front of the hills, faced the parade ground and the Missouri River beyond. After a short visit to Monroe, Libbie joined Custer at the fort.

Custer house (reconstruction), Fort Abraham Lincoln

June and July 1874

To have better control over Indians who had been raiding settlements in Nebraska, Sheridan intended to establish a new post on reservation lands in the vicinity of the Black Hills. Sheridan ordered Custer to lead an exploratory expedition into the area with a force comprising ten companies of the Seventh Cavalry, two infantry companies, and a group of civilians, including two miners to search for rumored gold in the hills. The expedition left Fort Lincoln on July 2, after receiving a shipment of Springfield carbines. The new single-shot carbines were to replace the troops' trusty seven-shot Spencers. This would be their first test in the field.

July 22, 1874

Custer skirted the Black Hills on the north side to enter them from the west. While the expedition was camped at the base of a mountain known as Inyan Kara, Custer climbed the 6,500-foot-high prominence and saw the pine-covered Black Hills close by to the east. To the west, in the crystalline air, prairie grasslands stretched to the distant Bighorn Mountains.

Inyan Kara Mountain, south of Sundance, Wyoming

Castle Valley, Black Hills National Forest, northwest of Deerfield, South Dakota

July 24-26, 1874

The expedition entered the Black Hills by way of a beautiful flower-carpeted valley, which Custer named Floral Valley. A few days later, deeper into the hills, the expedition came upon a lush valley surrounded by high limestone formations. Custer called the place Castle Valley.

Floral Valley, north of Buckhorn, Wyoming

July 31, 1874

As his men camped and the miners searched for gold, Custer climbed the highest mountain in the Black Hills, Harney Peak. At a height of 7,242 feet, the granite mass was a thousand or more feet higher than most of the other peaks in the area.

When Custer returned to camp, he found that the miners had discovered a small amount of gold.

Harney Peak, Black Hills National Forest

August 1 and 2, 1874

Custer established a permanent camp on French Creek. From there he could explore the hills while the miners searched for gold. The very next day, the prospectors made a worthwhile strike, and Custer dispatched one of his Indian scouts to carry the news to Fort Laramie, in Wyoming Territory. Although Custer emphasized that the worth of the strike would require further evaluation, the news leaked, and it made headlines in newspapers around the country.

French Creek, Black Hills National Forest, south of Custer, South Dakota

August 14, 1874

From his camp at Bear Butte, a mountain rising from a flat plain about ten miles northeast of the Black Hills, Custer sent a dispatch to Brig. Gen. Alfred H. Terry, commander of the Department of Dakota. He reported that the Black Hills were not impenetrable, and that he had entered from the west, explored south to where the hills ended at the south fork of the Cheyenne River, and headed northeast when he left them. He considered the area excellent for farming and stock raising because of the pure water and fine pasturage.

Bear Butte, Bear Butte State Park, east of Sturgis, South Dakota

September 1874 to October 1875

The Sioux were furious over the invasion of Custer and other whites into the Black Hills—a sacred place to them. They called Custer's route the Thieves' Road. According to the Treaty of 1868, government agents could have access to the lands, but other whites had to obtain the Indians' consent. After the gold was discovered, however, miners poured into the area without asking permission of anyone, and Sioux anger intensified. The government made a perfunctory effort to push the miners out, but it was unsuccessful, and soon the hills were overrun with gold seekers. Custer had hoped to be included in the forces sent to oust the miners from the Black Hills, but he was kept at Fort Lincoln. Except for drilling the troops and occasional scouting trips, Custer had little to do.

In the summer of 1875, the government tried to purchase the Black Hills from the Sioux, but the negotiations failed. One of the major obstacles was the stipulation that three-quarters of the male Sioux had to agree to the sale of any land. Since many Sioux were not on the reservation, no one knew how many men there were, or how to reach them.

Parade ground, Fort Abraham Lincoln, Mandan, North Dakota

December 1875 to May 1876

To gather enough male Sioux to discuss the sale of the Black Hills, President Grant and Generals Sherman and Sheridan sent word to the Indians to report to the reservation by the end of January. If they did not, they would be considered "hostiles" and the army would come after them. But at the appointed time, no Indians showed up. They sent word that deep snow had prevented them from coming. Most of them, however, had no intention of going to the reservation; as far as they were concerned, they were living peacefully and not bothering the whites.

To show the Indians that the government would brook no disobedience, Sheridan mounted a three-pronged offensive against them while it was still winter and their ponies were weak. Custer was to join the campaign, but in March, as he readied his regiment, he was summoned to Washington to testify before a congressional committee regarding Secretary of War William W. Belknap. Belknap was being investigated for taking kickbacks from post sutlers and Indian traders.

Custer had been vocal in his criticism of graft in the post sutlership at Fort Lincoln, and of the corruption at Indian agencies. After four weeks of testimony, during which questionable activities of Orvil Grant, the president's brother,

came under examination along with those of Belknap, the congressional committee determined to impeach Belknap. Custer was further detained to appear at the trial.

Impatient to return to Fort Lincoln, Custer appealed to Sherman for a release from testifying. His request was eventually forwarded to President Grant, who ignored it. Custer tried to plead his case in person, but the president would not see him. Custer suspected it was Grant's way of punishing him for making negative statements about him and his brother.

In early May, Custer went to St. Paul, Minnesota, to see General Terry at his headquarters. Grant sent orders for him to be arrested on the charge of leaving Washington without official release from the War Department. Custer, now desperate to get to Fort Lincoln before his regiment left, drafted a telegram to Grant to which both Terry and Sheridan added a personal endorsement. Grant relented, and Custer rejoined his regiment.

It was not sudden beneficence that caused Grant to change his mind. Custer was still a popular national figure, and newspapers had been criticizing Grant for mistreating him. Allowing Custer's request was a way to curry favor with the press.

Hills to the west, Fort Abraham Lincoln

May 17, 1876

At last, the campaign against the recalcitrant Indians was under way. With General Terry in command, the contingent from Fort Lincoln, including Custer leading the Seventh Cavalry, marched west, accompanied by the band playing "The Girl I Left Behind Me."

Custer campsite on Heart River

May 18, 1876

Libbie Custer had gone with her husband to the first night's camp on the Heart River. The next morning, their parting was more emotional than usual. Custer watched her as she rode to the crest of a small hill above the campsite. She paused to wave to him, then disappeared. Custer turned to his orderly and said, "A soldier has to serve two mistresses. While he's loyal to one, the other must suffer."

As Libbie made her way back to Fort Lincoln, her heart was heavy with a premonition of disaster.

Hill above Custer campsite on Heart River

Near Theodore Roosevelt National Park, Medora, North Dakota

— Eight —
FINAL CONFRONTATION
June 1876

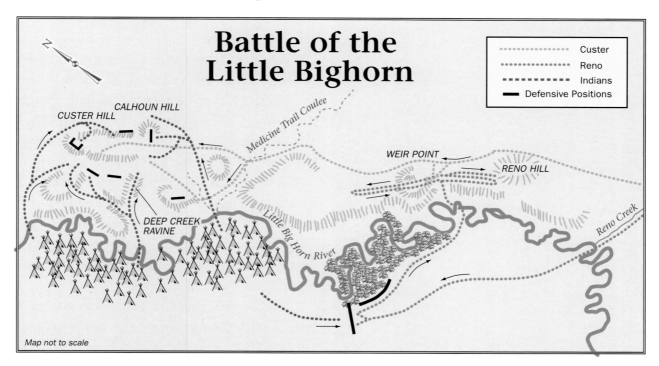

Battle of the Little Bighorn

Custer ....
Reno ....
Indians ▪▪▪▪▪▪▪▪
Defensive Positions ▬▬▬

CALHOUN HILL

CUSTER HILL

Medicine Trail Coulee

WEIR POINT

RENO HILL

DEEP CREEK RAVINE

Little Big Horn River

Reno Creek

Map not to scale

June 10-20, 1876

By the end of May, the expedition had reached the badlands of the Little Missouri River, in western Dakota Territory. They had encountered no Indians and had no accurate information about where the villages were. On

June 10 General Terry rode ahead to the Yellowstone River to meet with Col. John Gibbon from Fort Ellis, in Montana Territory. Custer was to take the supply wagons to the confluence of the Yellowstone and Powder Rivers, then join Terry and Gibbon upstream.

June 21, 1876

Custer found Terry and Gibbon at the mouth of the Rosebud River. At a meeting with the officers on the steamboat the *Far West,* Terry explained the strategy—a pincer movement to catch the Indians between two forces of the army. A large concentration of Sioux and Cheyenne was thought to be on the Bighorn River, south of the Yellowstone, but because the officers did not know the Indians' exact location, Gibbon was to march up the Yellowstone to the Bighorn, and if they were not there, go on to the Little Bighorn. Custer would follow the Rosebud River southwest to its headwaters, then turn west to join Gibbon at the Little Bighorn. Meanwhile, Brig. Gen. George Crook, then in northern Wyoming Territory, would move in from the south when he deemed the time was right.

Terry's orders gave Custer considerable latitude. They outlined the route he was to follow, but said: "It is, of course, impossible to give you any definite instructions in regard to this movement." Likewise, the orders stated the actions Custer was to take ". . . unless you see sufficient reason for departing from them."

Mouth of the Rosebud River, east of Forsyth, Montana

June 24, 1876

Custer came to a place where many Indian trails converged. His Crow Indian scouts determined that the Sioux and Cheyennes were preparing for a battle. Custer continued to follow the main trail toward the Little Bighorn. As the men set up camp for the night east of the divide between the Rosebud and Little Bighorn Rivers, Custer sent three scouts to continue tracking the Indians. At nine o'clock that night, they returned, reporting that they had not found the village, but that the trail was so fresh that an Indian camp must be nearby.

Two hours later, Custer ordered his men to break camp and move to the summit of the divide. He planned to wait there through the next day while the scouts reconnoitered the area, then launch a surprise attack at dawn the following day.

Sundance site, north of Lame Deer, Montana

*View from top of Crows Nest, southeast of Little Bighorn
Battlefield National Monument, Crow Agency, Montana*

June 25, 1876
5:00 A.M.*

Custer had sent several officers and Crow scouts to the top of the Crows Nest, a high butte overlooking the Little Bighorn Valley, to watch for signs of Indians. As dawn broke, they were astonished to see the largest horse herd they had ever beheld. For miles along the river, a gray haze from the smoke of what had to be hundreds of campfires blanketed the valley. As the scouts were on their way back to Custer, a party of six Sioux spotted them. The soldiers tried to catch the Indians, but the six galloped away toward the village.

---

* All times are the authors' estimates.

9:00 A.M.

Upon hearing the scouts' report, Custer climbed to the top of the Crows Nest to assess the situation. In the brighter daylight the smoke was not discernible, but Custer did see a large dust cloud. He thought that perhaps the six Sioux had given warning and the village was moving away.

10:30 A.M.

When Custer returned to the column, he learned that a squad of soldiers had backtracked to retrieve a box of hardtack that had fallen off a mule and found some Sioux breaking into it. The soldiers had fired at the warriors and chased them off. Now, with little chance of surprising the Indians, Custer believed he had to abandon his original plan and attack immediately.

12:00 NOON to 1:00 P.M.

Advancing down Ash (later named Reno) Creek, Custer ordered Capt. Frederick W. Benteen, with Companies D, H, and K, to scout to the south to find out whether the village was on the move and, if so, whether it was going north or south. Benteen was to move as quickly as possible, before the Indians could get away, and report back to Custer.

Former Ash Creek, now Reno Creek, southeast of Little Bighorn Battlefield

1:00 P.M. to 2:35 P.M.

Continuing forward, Custer's men came upon a single tipi containing the body of a Sioux warrior. Ahead they saw a cloud of dust kicked up by Indians fleeing at the sight of the soldiers. Custer knew these Indians would warn the village. He ordered Maj. Marcus A. Reno to take Companies A, G, and M across the Little Bighorn to attack the southern end of the village and run off the pony herd. In the meantime, with the five remaining companies, he would move concealed behind the bluffs on the east side of the river to the north end of the village, then cross the river and drive the Indians toward Reno. Companies C, E, F, I, and L were commanded respectively by Capt. Thomas Custer, Lt. Algernon E. Smith, Capt. George W. Yates, Capt. Miles W. Keogh, and Lt. James Calhoun. Custer planned for Benteen, whom he expected to rejoin him momentarily, to lead the center assault.

Vicinity of lone tipi site, southeast of Little Bighorn Battlefield

Site of Sioux and Cheyenne village on Little Bighorn River, from hill where Custer first saw it, Little Bighorn Battlefield

3:00 P.M.

From a hill, Custer saw Reno beginning his charge into the village, but curving bluffs blocked his view of the entire encampment. He sent Sgt. Daniel A. Kanipe with the order that the men bring up the pack train as quickly as possible.

Weir Point, where Custer viewed the entire Indian village, Little Bighorn Battlefield

3:15 P.M.

Atop a small, conical hill now known as Weir Point, Custer got a complete view of the Indian camp, which, he was dismayed to find, was huge, stretching for three miles along the river. He saw Reno fighting on foot under heavy fire and knew he had to attack quickly. Concerned that Benteen had not returned, he sent trumpeter John Martin to find him and bring him back immediately.

3:45 P.M.

Just east of the ford at Medicine Tail Coulee, five warriors fired on Custer. Halting briefly, hoping that Benteen would arrive, he dispatched Lieutenant Smith and Company E to give chase and to prevent other Indians from fording the creek. From a nearby ridge, Smith and his company poured heavy fire into the Indians, who were by now streaming across the ford.

Ford at Medicine Tail Coulee on Little Bighorn River, Little Bighorn Battlefield

3:55 P.M. to 4:30 P.M.

Reno and his men had been fighting a losing battle. Upon seeing hundreds of mounted warriors charging toward him, Reno pivoted his line of dismounted troopers into a wooded area on the bank of the river. A fierce fight ensued. Overwhelmingly outnumbered, Reno panicked and ordered his men to retreat across the river. The Indians pursued the soldiers as they scrambled up the steep bluff on the other side. At the top of the bluff, Reno, still under fire, set up a defensive position.

Benteen, having taken his time returning from his scout, now arrived on the scene. Reno had already lost almost half his men, and he beseeched Benteen to stay and help him. Benteen complied, ignoring Custer's order. Neither officer knew Custer's exact whereabouts, only that he was somewhere to the north, and Custer had no way of knowing about Reno's plight.

Site of Reno's retreat across the Little Bighorn River, Little Bighorn Battlefield

4:30 P.M.

Custer advanced a little over a mile along the crest of a ridge that ran north and south, today called Battle Ridge. Company F was in the lead, followed by C, E, and I, with L in the rear. The Indians pressed Custer's rear from the south, and Custer ordered Lieutenant Calhoun's Company L to dismount and form a rear-guard skirmish line along the ridge to stop them. At the same time, he ordered Company I, under Captain Keogh, to take a position behind Company L to prevent its being cut off.

Custer headed for a small hill—now known as Custer Hill—at the north end of the ridge, where steep slopes fell away to the east, west, and north. Here he intended to establish a defensive perimeter and hold out until Benteen arrived. Along the way, Cheyenne warriors, concealed in the tall grass, fired arrows at the soldiers, while others made their way through a ravine below.

Battle Ridge, Little Bighorn Battlefield

4:40 P.M.

Custer noticed another group of Cheyennes amassing northwest of Custer Hill. Worried they might cut him off, he deployed Companies C and E to hold them back and to flush others from the grass. Upon reaching the hill, Custer ordered the horses killed and used as barricades. Suddenly, howling Oglala Sioux warriors rushed up the hill from the north and east. Company F tried to repulse them.

Deep Ravine Trail, Little Bighorn Battlefield

Calhoun Hill, Little Bighorn Battlefield

4:55 P.M.

Calhoun's Company L, trying to hold the rear guard position, was completely over-whelmed by onrushing Hunkpapa Sioux.

Position of Keogh's company, Little Bighorn Battlefield

5:00 P.M.

Trying to reach Custer on the hill, Keogh and Company I fought off an onslaught of Indians from the south while Oglalas surged in from the north and trapped them. One concentrated volley from the Indians' guns demolished the entire troop.

5:05 P.M.

At the same time, Cheyennes from the northwest charged into the center of Companies C and E, scattering them into small, disorganized groups. Many of the troopers ran into a ravine to the west, Deep Ravine, where they soon met their end.

Deep Ravine, Little Bighorn Battlefield

Custer Hill, with grave markers,
Little Bighorn Battlefield

5:10 P.M.

Having wiped out all the other soldiers, the Indians concentrated their attention on the few men remaining with Custer atop the small hill.

5:30 P.M.

As Custer's troops ran out of ammunition and their Springfield carbines jammed, it was easy for the Indians to overrun them. In desperate hand-to-hand-combat, wielding their carbines as clubs, Custer and his men put up a courageous fight, but within minutes, every white man was dead.

Aftermath

Benteen and Reno had not yet set out to look for Custer. After hearing heavy firing, which he assumed was Custer engaging the Indians, the commander of Company D, Capt. Thomas D. Weir, felt he should find Custer immediately. He asked Reno's permission to reconnoiter to the north with his company, but Reno refused. Angered, Weir ordered his company to mount anyway and they rode off.

Twenty-five minutes after Weir left to find Custer, Benteen and three companies followed, with Reno and the other companies straggling behind. Benteen met Weir on the hill from which Custer had first glimpsed the Indian encampment (Weir Point). From there, Weir and Benteen saw a large body of Indians streaming in their direction. With dust and smoke obscuring much of the battlefield, they could see nothing of Custer's troops.

With ever-increasing numbers of Indians firing on them, Benteen and Reno retreated to a defensive position at the top of the bluff.

Throughout the night after the battle, Indians harassed Reno, Benteen, and their men and tried to prevent them from reaching the river—their only source of water. But by midafternoon the next day the Indians had gone.

On June 27, General Terry and Colonel Gibbon arrived from the north. Greeting their eyes was the grisly carnage on Custer Hill. The scattered bodies had been stripped; many were mutilated. Custer's body, unravaged, rested in a position of calm repose against two corpses.

The 212 men who died in the battle of the Little Bighorn were buried where they had fallen. Several years later, most of the enlisted men were reburied in a common grave under a monument erected on Custer Hill. A few were buried elsewhere.

View north from Weir Point toward Custer Hill, Little Bighorn Battlefield

In October 1877, Custer's body was interred at West Point. Fifty-six years after her husband's death, Libbie, his ardent champion until the end, died. She was laid to rest in a grave beside his.

GEORGE ARMSTRONG CUSTER
MAJOR GENERAL
U·S·VOL·

CUSTER

Graves of George and Elizabeth Custer, U.S. Military Academy cemetery, West Point, New York

Conclusion

For many years, Custer was to us just another figure in the panoply of history. Later, when we became interested in the history of the American West, specifically that regarding the Plains Indians, we learned more about Custer and the part he played in the Indian wars—according to many historians. These often portrayed Custer as arrogant, vainglorious, stupid, selfish, cruel, and even insane. Our initial opinion of Custer was formed from these writings, as we had not yet done research of our own.

As we began work on this book, we became fascinated with the enigmatic Custer, and now, after thoroughly researching his life, we have concluded that our original opinion of him was wrong. We have come to admire him. In fact, we think he was a remarkable fellow, which puts us at odds with a surprising number of people who have nothing good to say about him.

Those who belittle him often seize upon his standing at the bottom of his West Point class, or his court-martial, or his attacks on Indians as reasons to do so. We have found these arguments to be invalid. Custer may have been last in his class, but he was smart enough to pass his qualifying examinations and, four years later, to graduate with the class of 1862. Had he been a more diligent student, his ranking would undoubtedly have been higher.

As to Custer's court-martial, careful examination of the documented events leading up to it and the records of the trial proceedings show that most of those impaneled to judge Custer had reason to be prejudiced against him, and the charges, for the most part, were trumped up. The mild sentence he received—a year's suspension—reflects this.

Custer did attack Indians, but that was, after all, his job. In all instances he was acting under orders from his superiors, just as every military officer must do. Unlike many of those in the army, Custer had no hatred of Indians and was not bent on killing them indiscrimately. He was fair in his dealings with them, and in fact he rather envied their free way of life and felt some remorse that he was helping to destroy it. Custer was also disturbed by the Indian agents who regularly cheated the Indians, and he testified before a congressional committee on the issue.

Many of those who malign Custer base their opinions not on documented facts but on their own assumptions. Without benefit of research, they conjecture that he was a wanton Indian killer and a seeker of military glory whose tactics were reckless. Yet Custer's record in the Civil War, often overlooked by his critics, was extraordinary. He built his various commands into formidable fighting units and led them fearlessly into the fray.

Much of the criticism of Custer's actions in the Battle of the Little Bighorn fails to take into account that Custer had no reason to think the Indians would try to defend their position, as they normally fled when facing a large body of troops. While it's true that Custer made some serious errors in judgment, the fault for this military failure is not all his.

The reports of some of the officers who survived the battle cast Custer in a very poor light, but we must remember that they likely used the dead leader as a scapecoat to protect their own backsides.

Custer made some brilliant decisions and some awful mistakes. He had devoted friends and jealous enemies. Although he has become larger than life, ultimately he was a human being just like the rest of us.

Sites of Interest

KANSAS

Fort Harker Museum
  Kanopolis, Kansas
  785-472-5733

Fort Hays State Historic Site
  Hays, Kansas
  785-625-6812
  www.kshs.org/places/forthays/

Fort Larned National Historic Site
  Larned, Kansas
  620-285-6911
  nps.gov/fols

Fort Leavenworth Military Reservation
  Leavenworth, Kansas
  913-684-5604
  http://www.leavenworth.army.mil/cac/
    history.htm

Frontier Army Museum
  913-684-3767
  leavenworth.army.mil/museum

Fort Riley Military Reservation
  Custer House
  United States Cavalry Museum
  Fort Riley, Kansas
  785-239-2737
  www.riley.army.mil/Recreation/
    Museums.asp

Fort Wallace Museum
  Wallace, Kansas
  785-891-3564
  www.fortwallace.org

KENTUCKY

Elizabethtown Tourism and
Convention Bureau
  Elizabethtown, Kentucky
  800-437-0092
  www.touretown.com

MARYLAND

Antietam National Battlefield
  Sharpsburg, Maryland
  301-432-5124
  nps.gov/anti/home.htm

MICHIGAN

Monroe County Historical Museum
  Monroe, Michigan
  734-240-7780
  www.co.monroe.mi.us/Museum

MONTANA

Little Bighorn Battlefield
National Monument
  Crow Agency, Montana
  406-638-2621
  www.nps.gov/libi/index.htm

Pompeys Pillar National Monument
   Pompeys Pillar, Montana
   406-875-2233
   www.mt.blm.gov/pillarmon/general.html

NEW YORK

United States Military Academy
   West Point Museum
   West Point, New York
   845-938-2203/2638
   www.usma.edu/Museum

NORTH DAKOTA

Fort Abraham Lincoln State Park
   Mandan, North Dakota
   701-667-6340
   www.ndparks.com/parks/FLSP.htm

OHIO

Custer Monument and Museum
   New Rumley, Ohio
   740-945-6415
   www.ohiohistory.org/places/custer/

OKLAHOMA

Black Kettle Museum
   Cheyenne, Oklahoma
   580-497-3929
   nps.gov/waba/pphtml/facilities.html or
   www.cheyenneokchamber.com/
      blackkettlemuseum.htm

Fort Sill Military Reservation and
National Historic Landmark
   Fort Sill Museum
   Lawton, Oklahoma
   580-442-5123
   sill-www.army.mil/Museum/

Washita Battlefield National Historic Site
   Cheyenne, Oklahoma
   580-497-2742
   nps.gov/waba

PENNSYLVANIA

Gettysburg National Military Park
   Gettysburg, Pennsylvania
   717-334-1124
   nps.gov/gett

VIRGINIA

Appomattox Court House
National Historical Park
   Appomattox, Virginia
   434-352-8987
   www.nps.gov/apco

Belle Grove Plantation
   Middleton, Virginia
   540-869-2028
   bellegrove.org

Cedar Creek Battlefield
   Middleton, Virginia
   540-869-2064
   cedarcreekbattlefield.org

Colonial Williamsburg
   Williamsburg, Virginia
   800-447-8679
   colonialwilliamsburg.com

Culpeper County Chamber of Commerce
   Culpeper, Virginia
   1-888-285-7373
   www.culpepervachamber.com

Fredericksburg and Spotsylvania
County National Military Park
   Fredericksburg, Virginia
   540-371-0802
   www.nps.gov/frsp

Manassas National Battlefield Park
   Manassas, Virginia
   703-361-1339
   www.nps.gov/mana

Saylers Creek Battlefield
State Historical Park
   c/o Twin Lakes State Park
   Green Bay, Virginia
   434-392-3435
   www.dcr.state.va.us/parks/sailorcr.htm

Winchester-Frederick County
Convention and Visitor Bureau
   Winchester, Virginia
   800-662-1360
   visitwinchesterva.com

WEST VIRGINIA

Harpers Ferry National Historical Park
   Harpers Ferry, West Virginia
   304-535-6298
   nps.gov/hafe/home.htm

Acknowledgements

It goes without saying that we could not have produced this book without the assistance of a great many people. First and foremost is Bonnie Jensen. While we travel, she is our bulwark who stays put and takes care of forwarding our mail and messages.

We gleaned a wealth of information from knowledgeable and helpful personnel at sites in many states that have some connection with Custer. In alphabetical order they are: Antietam National Battlefield; Appomattox Court House National Historical Park; Black Hills National Forest; Fort Abraham Lincoln State Park; Fort Larned National Historic Site; Fort Leavenworth; Fort Hays State Historic Site; Fort Riley; Fredricksburg and Spotsylvania County National Military Park; Gettysburg National Military Park; Harpers Ferry National Historical Park; Little Bighorn Battlefield National Monument; Manassas National Battlefield Park; Petersburg National Battlefield; Theodore Roosevelt National Park; and the United States Military Academy.

We could not do our work without libraries, and we cannot praise librarians highly enough for the assistance they have given us. Our thanks to all the many individuals who generously provided us with information, who personally conducted us to places we wanted to photograph, and who own property that was connected with Custer who allowed us to photograph their homes or lands.

Special thanks to Jim Court, former superintendent, Little Bighorn Battlefield National Monument, who was a source of much information, and to the late Dr. Lawrence A. Frost, whose knowledge of all things concerning Custer was encyclopedic, and who graciously took the time to answer all our many questions.

This would not be complete without thanks to our editor, the diligent Gwen McKenna, and Kim Ericsson for applying her artistic talents to designing the book.

215

Bibliography

Ambrose, Stephen E. *Crazy Horse and Custer.* New York: Doubleday & Company, 1975.

Battles and Leaders of the Civil War. Vol. 3. New York: The Century Co., 1884.

Berthrong, Donald J. *The Southern Cheyennes.* Norman: University of Oklahoma Press, 1963.

Bourke, John G. *On the Border with Crook.* Reprint, Lincoln: University of Nebraska Press, 1971.

Bradley, James H. *The March of the Montana Column.* Norman: University of Oklahoma Press, 1961.

Brady, Cyrus Townsend. *Indian Fights and Fighters.* Reprint, Lincoln: University of Nebraska Press, 1971.

Brininstool, E. A. *Troopers with Custer.* Harrisburg, Pa.: Telegraph Press, 1952.

Brooke-Rawle, William. *Gregg's Cavalry Fight at Gettysburg.* Philadelphia: Allen, Lane & Scott Printers, 1884.

Burkey, Blaine. *Custer, Come at Once!* Hays, Kans.: Thomas More Preparatory School, 1976.

Camp, Walter. *Custer in '76.* Reprint, Provo, Utah: Brigham Young University Press, 1976.

Carroll, John M. *Custer's Cavalry Occupation of Hempstead and Austin, Texas.* Glendale, Calif.: Arthur Clarke, 1983.

Crackel, Theodore J. "Custer's Kentucky." *Filson Club History Quarterly* 48, no. 2 (April 1974).

Custer, Elizabeth B. *Boots and Saddles.* Reprint, Norman: University of Oklahoma Press, 1961.

——. *Following the Guidon.* New York: Harper & Row, 1890.

——. *Tenting on the Plains.* New York: Charles L. Webster & Company, 1889.

Custer, George Armstrong. *My Life on the Plains.* Reprint, Norman: University of Oklahoma Press, 1978.

——. *War Memoirs.* Galaxy Magazine 21 (March, April, May, and June 1876).

Dippie, Brian W., ed. *Nomad: George A. Custer in Turf, Field, and Farm Magazine.* Austin: University of Texas Press, 1980.

Edwards, William B. *Civil War Guns.* Harrisburg, Pa.: Stackpole Co., 1962.

Ege, Robert J. *Curse Not His Curls.* Ft. Collins, Colo.: Old Army Press, 1974.

Finerty, John F. *War-Path and Bivouac.* Reprint, Lincoln: University of Nebraska Press, 1966.

Foote, Shelby. *The Civil War: A Narrative, Fredricksburg to Meridian.* New York: Random House, 1963.

Fougera, Katherine Gibson. *With Custer's Cavalry.* Reprint, Lincoln: University of Nebraska Press, 1986.

Frederick County Civil War Centennial Commission. *Civil War Battles in Winchester and Frederick County, Virginia 1861–1865.* N.p., 1971.

Frost, Lawrence A. "Cavalry Action of the Third Day at Gettysburg: A Case Study." *Military Collector and Historian* 29, no. 4 (Winter 1977).

——. *The Court Martial of General George Armstrong Custer.* Norman: University of Oklahoma Press, 1968.

——. *The Custer Album.* New York: Bonanza Books, 1984.

——. *General Custer's Libbie.* Seattle: Superior Publishing Company, 1976.

Graham, W. A. *The Custer Myth.* New York: Bonanza Books, 1953.

Gray, John S. *Centennial Campaign.* Ft. Collins, Colo.: Old Army Press, 1976.

Grinnell, George Bird. *The Fighting Cheyennes.* Reprint, Norman: University of Oklahoma, 1956.

Hart, Herbert M. *Tour Guide to Old Forts of Montana, Wyoming and North and South Dakota.* Ft. Collins, Colo.: Old Army Press, 1980.

——. *Tour Guide to Old Forts of Texas, Kansas, Nebraska and Oklahoma.* Ft. Collins, Colo.: Old Army Press, 1981.

Hoig, Stan. *The Battle of the Washita.* New York: Doubleday & Company, 1976.

Hyde, George E. *A Life of George Bent.* Reprint, Norman: University of Oklahoma, 1968.

——. *Red Cloud's Folk.* Reprint, Norman: University of Oklahoma Press, 1975.

——. *Spotted Tail's Folk.* Reprint, Norman: University of Oklahoma, 1974.

Jackson, Donald. *Custer's Gold.* Reprint, Lincoln: University of Nebraska Press, 1972.

Josephy, Alvin M., Jr. *The Patriot Chiefs.* Reprint, New York: Viking Press, 1969.

Kidd, James H. *Personal Recollections of a Cavalryman.* Ionia, Mich.: Sentinel Printing Company, 1908.

Kinsley, D. A. *Favor the Bold.* 2 vols. New York: Holt, Rinehart & Winston, 1968.

Kuhlman, Charles. *Legend into History.* Harrisburg, Pa.: Stackpole Company, 1951.

Lee, William O. *Seventh Regiment, Michigan Volunteer Cavalry 1862–1865.* Detroit: Seventh Michigan Cavalry Association, n.d.

Mails, Thomas E. *Plains Indians, Dog Soldiers, Bear Men, and Buffalo Women.* Englewood Cliffs, N.J.: Prentice Hall, 1973.

Marquis, Thomas B. *Custer on the Little Bighorn.* Lodi, Calif.: Dr. Marquis Custer Publications, 1967.

——. *Keep the Last Bullet for Yourself.* New York: Two Continents Publishing Group, 1976.

——. *Wooden Leg: A Warrior Who Fought Custer.* Reprint, Lincoln: University of Nebraska Press, 1957.

McHenry, Robert, ed. *Webster's American Military Biographies.* Springfield, Mass.: G & C Merriam Company, 1978.

McLaughlin, James. *My Friend the Indian.* Seattle: Superior Publishing, 1970.

Mende, Fred. *Custer and the McLean House.* Appomattox Court House National Historic Park files, n.d.

Merington, Marguerite. *The Custer Story.* New York: Devin-Adair Company, 1950.

Mitchell, Joseph B. *Decisive Battles of the Civil War.* Reprint, New York: Fawcett Premier, 1955.

Moeller, Bill and Jan. *Crazy Horse: A Photographic Biography.* Missoula, Mont.: Mountain Press, 2000.

Monaghan, Jay. *Custer: The Life of General George Armstrong Custer.* Reprint, Lincoln: University of Nebraska Press, 1971.

Nelson, Bruce. *Land of the Dacotahs.* Reprint, Lincoln: University of Nebraska, n.d.

Nye, Wilbur Sturtevant. *Plains Indians Raiders.* Norman: University of Oklahoma Press, 1968.

Olson, James C. *History of Nebraska.* Lincoln: University of Nebraska Press, 1955.

Patterson, Gerard A. *Rebels from West Point.* New York: Doubleday & Company, 1987.

Potomac Corral of Westerners. *Great Western Indian Fights.* Reprint, Lincoln: University of Nebraska Press, 1966.

Price, William H. *A Civil War Handbook.* Fairfax, Va.: Prince Lithograph Co., 1961.

Progulske, Donald R., and Frank J. Shideler. *Following Custer.* Bulletin 674, Agricultural Experiment Station. Brookings: South Dakota State University, 1974.

Propst, Nell Brown. *Forgotten People: A History of the South Platte Trail.* Boulder, Colo: Pruett Publishing Co., 1979.

Quarles, Garland R. *Occupied Winchester 1861–1865.* Winchester, Va.: n.p., 1976.

———. *Some Old Houses in Frederick County, Virginia.* Winchester, Va.: Farmers & Merchants National Bank, 1971.

Reedstrom, Ernest L. *Bugles, Banners and War Bonnets.* New York: Bonanza Books, 1986.

Ricker, E. S. Tablet 13. Nebraska Historical Society, n.d.

Rister, Carl Coke. *Border Command: General Phil Sheridan in the West.* Norman: University of Oklahoma Press, 1944.

Robertson, James I., Jr. *Civil War Sites in Virginia.* Charlottesville: University Press of Virginia, 1982.

Root, Frank A., and William E. Connelley. *The Overland Stage to California.* Reprint, Columbus, Ohio: Long's College Book Co., 1950.

Sandoz, Mari. *The Battle of the Little Big Horn.* Reprint, Lincoln: University of Nebraska Press, 1978.

———. *Crazy Horse: The Strange Man of the Oglalas.* Reprint, Lincoln: University of Nebraska Press, 1961.

Schaff, Morris. *The Spirit of Old West Point: 1858–1862.* Boston: Houghton, Mifflin & Co., 1907.

Scudder, Ralph E. *Custer Country.* Portland, Ore.: Binfords & Mort, Publishers, 1963.

Shannon, Denise E. "Custer's Texas Home." *Texas Highways* (Feb 1986).

Simmons, Henry E. *A Concise Encyclopedia of the Civil War.* New York: Fairfax Press, 1986.

Steere, Edward. *Wilderness Campaign.* Harrisburg, Pa.: Stackpole Company, 1960.

Stevens, William Oliver. *Old Williamsburg and Her Neighbors.* New York: Dodd Mead & Co., 1938.

Stewart, Edgar I. *Custer's Luck.* Reprint, Norman: University of Oklahoma Press, 1955.

Symonds, Craig L. *A Battlefield Atlas of the Civil War.* Baltimore: Nautical & Aviation Publishing, 1983.

Taylor, Joseph H. "Inkpaduta and Sons." *North Dakota Historical Collection* 4, no. 3 (April 1930).

Terrell, John Upton, and George Walton. *Faint the Trumpet Sounds: The Life and Trial of Major Reno.* New York: David McKay Co., 1966.

Urwin, Gregory J. W. *Custer Victorious.* London: Associated University Presses, 1983.

Utley, Robert M. *Frontier Regulars.* New York: Macmillan Publishing Co., 1973.

———, ed. *Life in Custer's Cavalry.* New Haven, Conn.: Yale University Press, 1977.

Vestal, Stanley. *Warpath and Council Fire.* New York: Random House, 1948.

———. *Warpath: The True Story of the Fighting Sioux.* Reprint, Lincoln: University of Nebraska Press, 1984.

Wagner, Glendolin Damon. *Old Neutriment.* Reprint, Bryan, Texas: J. M. Carroll & Company, 1973.

War of the Rebellion: A Compilation of the Official Records of the Union and Confederate Armies. Washington, D.C.: Government Printing Office, 1880–1901.

Whittaker, Frederick. *A Complete Life of George A. Custer.* New York: Sheldon & Company, 1876.

Winchester: Battle Prize. Winchester, Va.: Winchester-Frederick County Chamber of Commerce, n.d.

Index

About the Authors

Husband and wife Bill and Jan Moeller are professional photographers and authors. Since 1982 they have traveled full-time in their RV to photograph historic sites around the United States. Having their home with them allows the Moellers to stay in an area as long as necessary to take pictures and do research for their unique photographic history books.

Before embarking on their land-based ventures, the Moellers lived aboard a sailboat for twelve years, touring the Atlantic Coast. In addition to their photo histories, the authors have published books and articles on sailing and RV travel.

Other Moeller photographic history books published by Mountain Press include:

Chief Joseph and the Nez Perces:
A Photographic History
(ISBN 0-87842-319-2)

Lewis and Clark: A Photographic Journey
(ISBN 0-87842-405-9)

Crazy Horse: A Photographic Biography
(ISBN 0-87842-424-5)

The Oregon Trail: A Photographic Journey
(ISBN 0-87842-442-3)

The Pony Express: A Photographic History
(ISBN 0-87842-470-9)

We encourage you to patronize your local bookstore. Most stores will order any title that they do not stock. You may also order directly from Mountain Press using the order form provided below or by calling our toll-free number and using your credit card. We will gladly send you a complete catalog upon request.

Some other titles of interest:

_____The Arikara War: *The First Plains Indian War, 1823*	$18.00/paper	$30.00/cloth
_____The Bloody Bozeman: *The Perilous Trail to Montana's Gold*	$28.00/paper	
_____Chief Joseph and the Nez Perces: *A Photographic History*	$15.00/paper	
_____Christmas in the Old West: *A Historical Scrapbook*	$16.00/paper	
_____Crazy Horse: *A Photographic Biography*	$20.00/paper	
_____Custer: *A Photographic Biography*	$24.00/paper	
_____Encyclopedia of Indian Wars: *Western Battles and Skirmishes, 1850–1890*		$28.00/cloth
_____The Journals of Patrick Gass: *Member of the Lewis and Clark Expedition*	$20.00/paper	
_____Lakota Noon: *The Indian Narrative of Custer's Defeat*	$18.00/paper	$36.00/cloth
_____Lewis & Clark: *A Photographic Journey*	$18.00/paper	
_____The Mystery of E Troop: *Custer's Gray Horse Company at the Little Bighorn*	$18.00/paper	$36.00/cloth
_____The Oregon Trail: *A Photographic Journey*	$18.00/paper	
_____The Piikani Blackfeet: *A Culture Under Siege*	$18.00/paper	$30.00/cloth
_____The Pony Express: *A Photographic History*	$22.00/paper	
_____Sacagawea's Son: *The Life of Jean Baptiste Charbonneau* (for readers 10 and up)	$10.00/paper	
_____The Saga of the Pony Express	$17.00/paper	$29.00/cloth
_____Stories of Young Pioneers: *In Their Own Words* (for readers 10 and up)	$14.00/paper	
_____William Henry Jackson: *Framing the Frontier*	$22.00/paper	$36.00/cloth

Please include $3.00 for 1-4 books or $5.00 for 5 or more books for shipping and handling.

Send the books marked above. I enclose $_____

Name_____

Address_____

City/State/Zip_____

☐ Payment enclosed (check or money order in U.S. funds)

Bill my: ☐ VISA   ☐ MasterCard   ☐ American Express   ☐ Discover   Exp. Date:_____

Card No._____

Signature_____

MOUNTAIN PRESS PUBLISHING COMPANY
P. O. Box 2399 • Missoula, MT 59806 • fax: 406-728-1635
Order Toll Free 1-800-234-5308 • Have your credit card ready.
e-mail: info@mtnpress.com • website: www.mountain-press.com